T0358716

We've Scene it All Before

TRANSGRESSIONS: CULTURAL STUDIES AND EDUCATION

Scope

Cultural studies provides an analytical toolbox for both making sense of educational practice and extending the insights of educational professionals into their labors. In this context *Transgressions: Cultural Studies and Education* provides a collection of books in the domain that specify this assertion. Crafted for an audience of teachers, teacher educators, scholars and students of cultural studies and others interested in cultural studies and pedagogy, the series documents both the possibilities of and the controversies surrounding the intersection of cultural studies and education. The editors and the authors of this series do not assume that the interaction of cultural studies and education devalues other types of knowledge and analytical forms. Rather the intersection of these knowledge disciplines offers a rejuvenating, optimistic, and positive perspective on education and educational institutions. Some might describe its contribution as democratic, emancipatory, and transformative. The editors and authors maintain that cultural studies helps free educators from sterile, monolithic analyses that have for too long undermined efforts to think of educational practices by providing other words, new languages, and fresh metaphors. Operating in an interdisciplinary cosmos, Transgressions: Cultural Studies and Education is dedicated to exploring the ways cultural studies enhances the study and practice of education. With this in mind the series focuses in a non-exclusive way on popular culture as well as other dimensions of cultural studies including social theory, social justice and positionality, cultural dimensions of technological innovation, new media and media literacy, new forms of oppression emerging in an electronic hyperreality, and postcolonial global concerns. With these concerns in mind cultural studies scholars often argue that the realm of popular culture is the most powerful educational force in contemporary culture. Indeed, in the twenty-first century this pedagogical dynamic is sweeping through the entire world. Educators, they believe, must understand these emerging realities in order to gain an important voice in the pedagogical conversation.

Without an understanding of cultural pedagogy's (education that takes place outside of formal schooling) role in the shaping of individual identity--youth identity in particular--the role educators play in the lives of their students will continue to fade. Why do so many of our students feel that life is incomprehensible and devoid of meaning? What does it mean, teachers wonder, when young people are unable to describe their moods, their affective affiliation to the society around them. Meanings provided young people by mainstream institutions often do little to help them deal with their affective complexity, their difficulty negotiating the rift between meaning and affect. School knowledge and educational expectations seem as anachronistic as a ditto machine, not that learning ways of rational thought and making sense of the world are unimportant.

But school knowledge and educational expectations often have little to offer students about making sense of the way they feel, the way their affective lives are shaped. In no way do we argue that analysis of the production of youth in an electronic mediated world demands some "touchy-feely" educational superficiality. What is needed in this context is a rigorous analysis of the interrelationship between pedagogy, popular culture, meaning making, and youth subjectivity. In an era marked by youth depression, violence, and suicide such insights become extremely important, even life saving. Pessimism about the future is the common sense of many contemporary youth with its concomitant feeling that no one can make a difference.

If affective production can be shaped to reflect these perspectives, then it can be reshaped to lay the groundwork for optimism, passionate commitment, and transformative educational and political activity. In these ways cultural studies adds a dimension to the work of education unfilled by any other sub-discipline. This is what Transgressions: Cultural Studies and Education seeks to produce—literature on these issues that makes a difference. It seeks to publish studies that help those who work with young people, those individuals involved in the disciplines that study children and youth, and young people themselves improve their lives in these bizarre times.

We've Scene it All Before

Using Film Clips in Diversity Awareness Training

Brian C. Johnson
Bloomsburg University

SENSE PUBLISHERS
ROTTERDAM/BOSTON/TAIPEI

A C.I.P. record for this book is available from the Library of Congress.

ISBN: 978-94-6091-020-3 (paperback)
ISBN: 978-94-6091-092-0 (hardback)
ISBN: 978-94-6091-022-7 (e-book)

Published by: Sense Publishers,
P.O. Box 21858, 3001 AW
Rotterdam, The Netherlands
http://www.sensepublishers.com

Printed on acid-free paper

This book is dedicated to every ordinary citizen who has taken up the charge in creating a better society. Keep loving; keep standing up; keep sitting in; keep speaking your mind. Your labor is not in vain.

TABLE OF CONTENTS

Chapter 1. Diversity Facilitation 1

Chapter 2. Best Practices in Diversity Education....................................11

Chapter 3. Raising Awareness of Difference, Power,
and Discrimination...19

Chapter 4. Film Clips..25

References 109

Index..111

DIVERSITY FACILITATION

Tips for the Novice Trainer

In an increasingly global and diverse society, it is crucial for citizens to learn about and express their emotions about issues relating to diversity, including race, ethnicity, gender and gender identity, sexual orientation and sexual identity, ability, age, religion, and socioeconomic class. Many people internalize anger, fear, contempt, and guilt about these issues. As a result, people express them in unhealthy and unproductive ways in school and the workplace. Diversity training addresses these emotions and behaviors; it provides a place for them to ask questions, make mistakes, be confronted, corrected (if necessary), and overcome inappropriate actions. Enter the diversity trainer.

Diversity trainers and facilitators are integral parts of any group discussing diversity issues. They organize, arrange, and lead different activities, such as discussions or quizzes that explore the many facets of diversity and multiculturalism. Trainers focus the discussion on specific issues, clarify main ideas and points of disagreement, and ask probing questions to expand the group's understanding. In addition, facilitators set and enforce ground rules to be followed during the discussion. By enforcing the guidelines governing the dialogue, they help determine the mood of the group and the overall effectiveness of the activities. The ground rules allow for more open and free communication of ideas and help participants feel more comfortable expressing themselves.

A discussion on the role of the diversity trainer should examine the etymology of the word "trainer." Its origin means "to drag" or "to pull" (Bee, 1998, p. 1). Certainly this conjures up a familiar image for those who have been involved in company-sponsored, mandatory (oft called "strongly encouraged") diversity training programs. Generally speaking, few employees fancy attending required programs no matter the professional development benefits; when the topic is diversity, the push, pull, drag, or tow analogy becomes quite vivid. This phenomenon, in part, results from reactionary diversity education—programs that are offered only after a problem or incident has occurred in the workplace. Those directly involved in the incident become the targets of the ire of the entire group as they get blamed for the mandatory meeting. Another scenario is more personal—sides are drawn as the friends of the perpetrator and victim divide the room and the facilitator becomes arbitrator rather than educator or trainer.

For the better part of the last two decades, businesses and other corporations have attempted to quell cultural disagreements in the workplace by offering diversity training. These often mandated programs offered little more than platitudes about sensitivity, and after that hour or two (or even a full day if there is a progressive organization) nothing had changed, except employees could check off that they had attended.

The diversity trainer was often unskilled at the art of facilitation, especially related to engaging difficult conversations and heated moments which had been raised by the conflicts and tensions of diversity engagement. This person often faced snarls, eye rolls, disrespect, and other methods of non-compliance. There were three types of diversity presenters; the first were those who were generalists in human resources and had little experience with real workplace diversity issues other than compliance with AA/EEO guidelines. Their typical program focus was to make it all go away. The second trainer was a hired specialist who came to the organization as an invited know-it-all dignitary who had some type of canned program that was rarely useful to the organization. The third, and probably most dangerous and ineffective, was the person who was selected simply for "being" diverse; this token individual was often angry and weary and whose in-your-face approach was simply to make persons from majority identities feel badly. For too many years organizations have relied on the diversity trainer to simply fix the issues surrounding issues of difference, rather than strategizing with the members of the workplace to enhance the inclusivity of the workplace.

Fortunately, there has been a paradigmatic shift from mere diversity training to more education around issues of systemic organizational change that both raises awareness and competencies, but also focuses on increasing opportunities for cross cultural dialogue skills development which leads to genuinely diverse and hospitable working atmospheres. This cultural shift, then, requires diversity trainers to become masterful at facilitation, which includes the skills of inclusion, communication, refereeing, and designing learning outcomes. Trainer-educators must have multiple methodologies to engage participants, and the primary objective of this resource is to provide the tools necessary to utilize the medium of mainstream Hollywood film as a part of instructional pedagogy.

Film is a useful vehicle for creating opportunities for participants and learners to discuss important topics. For many years, educators and other human services professionals, pastors and Christian educators have used movies in classrooms and other areas. Titles such as *Cinemeducation: a Comprehensive Guide to Using Film in Medical Education* (Alexander, Lenahan, & Pavlov, 2005), *Videos that Teach (v. 1-5)* (Fields & James, 1999, 2002, 2004, 2006) *Seeing Anthropology: Cultural Anthropology through Film* (Heider, Blakely, & Blakely, 2006), *Movie Clips for Kids: Faith-Building Video Devotions* (Cartwright, Cory, Kershner, Lavender, & Halasz, 2001), *Movie Based Illustrations for Preaching and Teaching* (Larson & Zahn, 2003), and *Reel Diversity: a Teacher's Sourcebook* (Johnson & Blanchard, 2008) reflect the power of this medium for instruction. The corporate arena has picked up on the value of using film in professional development programs; titles such as *Energizing Staff Development Using Film Clips: Memorable Movie Moments that Promote Reflection, Conversation, and Action* (Sommers & Olsen, 2005), *Our Feature Presentation: Management* (Champoux, 2003), *101 Movie Clips that Teach and Train* (Pluth, Wheeler, & Majeres, 2007), *Reel Lessons in Leadership* (DiSibio, 2006), and *Movies to Manage By* (Clemons & Wolff, 1999) have attempted to bring film into the corporate training venue; each has stressed film's values of convenience, audience familiarity and engagement, flexibility of usage, and the ability to capture real-life images in a timely manner.

FACILITATION SKILLS

During diversity programs, the facilitators should incorporate all participants of the group, as best as they are able. This includes allowing for disparate opinions that may seem antithetical to the gathering. Establishing a comfortable and trusting atmosphere allows people to openly express their thoughts, beliefs, and values. By asking questions about these thoughts, the trainers bring the group to the next level of understanding. Trainers must react to group members with empathy, compassion, and sensitivity.

Trainers must remain neutral during the discussion and refrain from expressing beliefs and opinions (this is a challenge sometimes). They must be aware of their areas of expertise, the limits of their knowledge, and their strengths and weaknesses as a leader as well as how these characteristics may influence their neutrality. During moments of conflict, tension, and controversy, facilitators must keep themselves calm and not take remarks personally. They must place the needs of the group before their own.

Checklist for Facilitators

1. Remain neutral and calm, while keeping personal opinions to you.
2. Set and enforce guidelines and ground rules for the group.
3. Focus and determine specific goals for the discussion.
4. Ask probing questions to expand the understanding of group members.
5. Show empathy and compassion to participants by acknowledging and validating their feelings.
6. Incorporate the use of activities and other techniques to engage group members.
7. Summarize key topics, points of conflict, and areas of agreement.
8. Put the needs of the group before your own.
9. Correct any misinformation.

Training sessions typically consist of three sections. During the beginning part, group members to one another, and provide background information on the specific topic to be discussed during the group. The middle section of the training or discussion consists of the "meat" of the program where material and information are disseminated. Facilitators should summarize key points and action items for future development.

Assessing Risk

Important to the learning process for participants is the ability of the facilitator to assess risk of the activities. Risk can be defined as the amount of tension and anxiety that the participants experience, which can fluctuate during the session. Different exercises require the participants to reveal different opinions and values, which may make some people feel uncomfortable. As the risk level increases, more discomfort may increase the likelihood of conflict within the group. Therefore, one major component to designing and facilitating a group involves controlling for and monitoring the risk level of the activities.

During the initial part of the session, try to keep the risk level at low. Participants may be unfamiliar with one another or are unsure of what to expect from the group (risk may be low, but anxiety may be slightly elevated). They may not be willing or comfortable to disclose personal information or opinions surrounding sensitive issues because they do not trust one another. To build this confidence, trainers use introductions and emotionally non-attached activities designed to foster a sense of community.

The overall risk level increases in the middle portion of the group session when the group focuses on the main goal or objective. Activities broach the subject at low risk to introduce the topic, but risk and discomfort increases as the topic is further explored. By this point in the session, group members share a sense of community and some degree of trust in each other. As a result, although the risk level is higher, they are more willing to express their true opinions and beliefs.

At the conclusion of the dialogue or event, the facilitator reduces the risk level by summarizing and debriefing. The trainer calms emotions and brings a sense of empowerment to the group. Any tensions or conflicts are reduced or aired. Experienced facilitators understand the importance of resolving tensions before the conclusion of the program for two reasons: 1) the attendee will have positive psychological resolution, and 2) encourages additional learning.

Each technique used in the three sections must be assessed for their risk level. If the activity requires participants to reveal sensitive or controversial personal information, the activity should be used in the middle of the section when trust and comfort are highest, in order to buffer the high risk level. Activities that require generic and widely accepted knowledge contain a lower risk and should be used at the beginning of the session or at the end.

Beginning a Training Session

Guidelines The first step in conducting a discussion or activity on diversity establishes the rules or general principles that shape the conversation. To keep a discussion from escalating to a high staked emotional debate or from falling into a rut of non-personal discussion, participants must listen to one another, be honest, and approach topics with an open mind. To help foster this type of environment, the ground rules build a framework for trust and camaraderie between the participants.

A list of suggested guidelines is included later in this manual. However, some groups may feel the need to add or remove rules. The list should reflect the needs and values of the participants. Because groups differ, the ground rules are individualized and specific to each session. In addition, during the activity, feel free to revise the list to accommodate for unforeseen needs. The list is not static, but rather a constant evolving basis for discussion.

Facilitators distribute copies of the guidelines to all individuals in the session; or, they may also hang up a copy of them in a centrally located position to remind participants what they are. The rules are read, discussed, explained if necessary, and revised. Clarify any questions from group members. The group comes to mutual agreement to abide by the guidelines.

During the session, facilitators must enforce the guidelines and directly address behaviors or events that do not abide by the rules. If participants break the rules, trainers use their judgment to address either the individual or the group. Usually, if the offense involved one or two people, trainers should approach the people on an individual and private basis. However, if the behavior influenced the majority of the group, then facilitators address the issue with the group.

Ice Breakers

Icebreakers provide group members a chance to get to know each other and build a sense of trust and camaraderie between individuals. In some groups, the participants may not know or have limited knowledge of each other. In some cases, talking specifically about diversity concepts and issues reveal unknown ideas or facts, even between individuals who have long term relationships. To create a trusting and honest atmosphere, which is necessary for effective dialogue, trainers provide activities for individuals to meet and greet each other.

The goal of these initial activities maximizes interaction among the group members. Wearing name tags allows people to respectfully communicate with each other, even if they do not know who they are. Introducing oneself in front of the group also helps people to attach names and faces. Another technique commonly used is to place people in dyads or triads. In these groups, the participants exchange names and one or more facts about themselves. For example, a person might reveal an affinity for playing the trumpet. Facilitators may ask the groups questions about defining diversity, the prevalence of one of the negative –isms, or a topic directly related to the topic of the day. Also, individuals may ask questions of the other people in the group to try to gather more information about them.

Following the small group interactions, the participants reconvene in the larger group. In some sessions, each group introduces themselves, tells about the other people in the group, and answers the questions posed by the facilitator. This technique ensures that the people in the group truly listened to one another, provides everyone with more information, and keeps the risk level relatively low.

Information

Because group members have varying levels of interest, experience, and knowledge about diversity, facilitators must provide information to the participants to establish a common foundation of understanding. Facilitators may present the objective or main focus of the group discussion by asking participants to read recent media articles about the topic. In addition, definitions or discussions to clarify definitions of ideas such as diversity, prejudice, etc., allow participants to enter into the discussion with common information.

Trainers often provide news articles, current events, or statistics to educate participants on the topics to be discussed. Also, definitions and terminology are stated and clarified through discussion or word-lists.

Facilitators also set goals for the dialogue group. These goals may range from increasing awareness of certain populations in a region, reducing interracial hostility, devising plans to combat classroom prejudice, or other topics. According to Ronald Hyman in *Improving Discussion Leadership* (1980), there are five types of discussions:

1. **Policy Discussion**. Examine and develop perspectives on a policy question, such as affirmative action.
2. **Problem-Solving Discussion**. Try to find answers to some problem.
3. **Explaining Discussion**. Analyze the causes and logic of a situation.
4. **Predicting Discussion**. Try to predict possible repercussions of a situation.
5. **Debriefing Discussion**. Examine and think about information gained from some activity.

Clearly stating the objectives of the group and explaining that the exercises and information used in the group support these efforts gives the group a unifying theme and focus. Therefore, all participants enter the group on a more common footing.

The Meat in the Middle

Address Main Focus   Once the goals and objective of the discussion or session are in place, conversation and activity begins. Maintaining a focused and progressive discussion requires careful monitoring and intervention. Timing is very important to the effectiveness of a discussion. The most controversial of topics should only be addressed after the participants build trusting relationships with each other and feel comfortable with one another. In addition, when these topics are presented, they need to be placed in context so that individuals are not caught off-guard.

While there are many techniques and structures for discussions, trainers must evaluate the risk level and applicability of each method in the group. Using high-risk exercises, such as presenting pornographic material to display the exploitation of women, should not be used in the beginning of the discussion because participants may feel uneasy about the material and refrain from participating in the discussion. Some exercises may be more useful in certain groups than others. For example, a trainer may decide to use the pornographic material in a group of college students, but not high school students or professional colleagues. Finally, the most effective dialogues begin with individual experiences, and then move outwards into community issues and the world around us.

One way to begin a discussion involves question and answers about the group members' personal experiences. Trainers pose open-ended questions that participants easily understand but that require multiple answers. However, to avoid catching the participants off guard, initial questions should keep the risk level low and slowly build up. For example, if discussing racial privilege, a facilitator might ask the group, "If you are left handed, what are some of the implicit disadvantages that a left-handed person faces? What are some of the privileges to being right-handed?" Using the topic of dominant-handedness maintains a low risk level while introducing the topic of privilege. Afterwards, the facilitators raise the risk level by posing the question, "What are some of the understood privileges of being white?" Tapping into racial identities, the trainer elevates the risk level and brings the group further into the dialogue.

During question/answer sections, trainers should pay close attention to the interactions between participants. They make sure that all participants have the opportunity to speak, that one or two individuals do not dominate the conversation, and that any misinformation or stereotypes are pointed out and corrected. Facilitators often probe learners for more information into their perspective by asking them to clarify, explain, or provide more specific examples. This helps group members understand different perspectives.

Another lower risk technique used in dialogues involves storytelling. Everyone has a story to tell-a variety of anecdotes from their history that they can feel comfortable and safe to contribute to group discussions. Sharing personal stories allows individuals to control the amount of information they reveal to the other group members while increasing the trust and camaraderie between the participants. People can identify with different components of the story and experience similar emotions as the storyteller. In addition, because diversity work requires people to address their own views about topics and to possibly rethink these perspectives, personally connecting with stories brings abstract ideas into reality and practicality.

Stories about childhood, school, religious practices, social and work situations, and families expose other group members to different behaviors and cultural practices. It allows the participants to compare their lives and reactions to similar situations to the person telling the story. Vocalizing and discussing these comparisons either as a large group or in smaller subunits provides individuals with exposure and knowledge about culture. Participants can ask questions about practices they do not understand or need further explanation.

Activities such as handouts, quizzes, videos, etc. may also be used. However, both before and after using these materials, facilitators should apply them to the dialogue topic. Each activity should be contextualized and its relevance explained. For example, if viewing a film, trainers should give a brief introduction about what the film depicts, point out key issues for group members to pay attention to, and pose questions for the group to keep in mind while watching the film. Afterwards, trainers often summarize the objective of the film or ask participants to identify the main idea of the film. Any questions initially posed are discussed. In addition, facilitators provide students with the opportunity to discuss any interesting or poignant issues from the film. By framing the film and giving the group direction, trainers increase the effectiveness of the activity in addressing the discussion topic.

Checklist and Tools for Main Topic Focus

1. Keep the discussion focused on the main objective and be ready to redirect the conversation.

2. Evaluate the timing, risk level, and appropriateness of each method used.
3. Ask probing, open-ended questions that allow students to further explore topics.
4. Use storytelling to engage all participants.
5. Use question and answer methods to investigate different perspectives.
6. Use films, videos, or other multimedia presentations, discussing their relevance to the topic both before and after the presentation.
7. Use quizzes and other handouts to further explain or induce conversation.
8. Provide participants with activities that involve individual work, small group work, and the group as a whole.

Hot Moments

Hot moments are times within the discussion when emotional tensions peak and conflicts occur. Some stereotypes and assumptions spark these moments. Because the diversity dialogues explore sensitive personal opinions and identities, people often become defensive and personalize comments. Hot moments are inevitable; however, by carefully managing them, facilitators turn the conflicts into learning opportunities. Some trainers view these uncomfortable times as the turning point in the group when the most work and learning occurs. They open up areas in the discussion that were previously avoided or overlooked, allowing a more in-depth examination of the relevant topic.

At the first sign of offensive remarks and hot moments, facilitators must stay calm and take leadership of the situation. By appearing un-shaken, facilitators provide a sense of stability, reaffirming the safe atmosphere of the group and allowing the students to explore the topic. In addition, remaining calm provides the group members with a model for their reactions and behaviors.

Facilitators acknowledge the tension in the group and address it immediately. Many trainers find it helpful to pause for a moment or two, allowing the participants to process the conflict and logically reason it *out*. Silence also provides the trainers with an opportunity to collect their thoughts on the issues, to distance themselves from the situation and take an objective viewpoint, as well as to try to understand the student's opinion or bias. In some situations, participants are unable to articulate their true emotions and opinions. Trainers look for the underlying meanings and subtext of people's comments to focus on the true conflict being encountered.

After recognizing the tensions, facilitators bring the issue to the forefront of conversation. If a particular group member made an offensive comment, the trainer takes the focus away from the student and generalizes the offense. For example, a facilitator might respond to a racist comment by saying, "Many people think this way. Why do they believe this? What causes them to think this way? On the other hand, why do other people not think this way?" This strategy tries to prevent personal attacks on the individual who made the comment and encourages other students who may feel similarly to anonymously express their views.

To resolve or to reduce the conflict during hot moments, information and perspectives on both sides of the issue must be presented. Often, tensions result from ignorance or miscommunication. Talking about why people hold certain beliefs and practices and exploring the motivations behind them raises awareness and understanding. Trainers sometimes have students listen to the other point of views on issues and then restate or defend the main idea of the argument that they originally disagreed with. This technique, effective for the most sensitive subjects, forces students to truly listen and comprehend what the other person says as well as process it for themselves before restating it in their own words.

In situations where participants are visibly shaken and upset, trainers provide the participants with the option of leaving the room to take a break. However, in any event where a person leaves the group, facilitators talk with the individuals privately outside the room. Through one on one interaction, the facilitator shows empathy and concern for the participant, validating her/his feelings. In addition, the trainer helps the person to learn something about self, other people, or the topic in general.

When hot moments and conflict arise, as they inevitably will, trainers directly confront the issue or offensive remark. Trainers think rationally, remain neutral, and find teaching opportunities in the occurrence. However, if a trainer cannot find a workable position in the conflict, s/he recognizes it but puts it to the side for later possessing. The deferment allows both the facilitator and the participants to calm down and plan strategies to effectively confront the topic. Before the end of the session, the group returns to the moment and deals with it, exploring the differing viewpoints surrounding it.

No Hot Moment is Ignored or Not Discussed

Trainer's checklist for dealing with hot moments

1. Acknowledge and either immediately confront the hot moment or agree to return to it later.
2. Stay calm and think rationally to find the learning opportunities in the conflict.
3. Take a few minutes to reflect on the moment and allow participants to process the tension.
4. Look for the underlying meanings of people's comments to find the focus of the issue at hand.
5. Enforce the ground rules to prevent personal attacks on participants.
6. Take the focus off the individual by generalizing her/his statement.
7. Have group members present differing viewpoints and the rationales behind them.
8. Have group members restate and defend conferring perspectives.
9. Talk with upset students individually.

Action

At the end of diversity training groups, participants often feel empowered and want to take action on a more community-based, broad level. Facilitators provide individuals with resources, ideas, and possible tools that they can use to continue their work on diversity issues. Arming learners with the techniques necessary to continue their work increases the likelihood of action.

For example, by providing a list of web sites related to the topic discussed, participants have the chance to further examine the dialogue topic, looking at new points of view. Many trainers also provide a suggested reading list with titles of relevant books, magazines, or journal articles that participants can read to further their understanding about diversity.

Ending a Training

Summarize and Debriefing   Before the conclusion of the discussion group, facilitators involve the group in a final summation and wrap-up of the discussion's events and findings. Bringing together the key points and highlighting the progression of the group's views causes participants to feel the discussion was effective and productive. When individuals feel that their efforts were valuable, they are more likely to continue to participate in diversity discussions as well as to work to raise awareness about issues.

During this time, any deferred hot moments are addressed, last questions are answered, and materials distributed. Facilitators closely monitor both the verbal and nonverbal communication signals of the group to identify any unresolved tensions, ambiguities, or emotions. Participants should leave the session without anger or unaired conflicts. Trainers debrief and assist individuals in calming down any emotions by allowing them time for final reflection, either in small groups or as a whole unit. In addition, some facilitators find it helpful to have groups identify and write about what they felt was important about the session or what they learned from it.

The role of the facilitator for diversity engagement is not an easy one, but with the right tools, facilitators and trainers can be quite successful in helping organizations and individuals in their strategic endeavors for planning, preparing, and promoting diversity and inclusion. In the later chapters, we will examine the film medium as one of these tools. Chapters will explore some core concepts of media literacy that are requisite to using this method, and best practice skills diversity education, cross cultural development, and inclusionary practice. The highlight of this resource is the chapter detailing scenes from feature length mainstream Hollywood films which provide visual example of twenty five terms which are essential to raising awareness of difference in the workplace.

BEST PRACTICES IN DIVERSITY EDUCATION

Tried and True Strategies

As a professional, are you committed to the development of a culturally inclusive work environment where the cultural identities of its constituents are affirmed? Do you endeavor to work at an institution where each community member feels liberated to be a whole person and has the freedom to critically explore and examine their own and others' opinions, beliefs, attitudes, and identities in a supportive environment? Do you uphold a firm commitment to diversity and recognize that there are multiple dimensions of diversity including, but not limited to, culture, race, ethnicity, nationality, geographical locations, age, sexuality and sexual orientation, ability, socioeconomic status, gender, class, linguistics, and religion? Are you equally committed to the values of social justice and creating equity and access for underrepresented and marginalized groups?

These are the central questions for the preparation, practice, and promotion of diversity and inclusiveness in your workplace. As you develop interactive diversity workshops, challenge the participants to understand the organizational and community benefits of a climate of *critical multiculturalism* (May, 1999; Goldberg, 2009; Steinberg, 2009). This includes the notion that creating a multicultural organization is an important component of any business enterprise, as it helps to build critical thinking and decision-making skills, and it provides opportunities for intercultural and cross-cultural interactions and relationship building. Having a diverse organization does not mean lowering standards or expectations, nor is it being concerned with being "politically correct." In fact, critical multiculturalism welcomes the vantage points of all members of the community and only seeks to ensure that *minority* groups have the equitable opportunity to be full-fledged members of the community.

Organizations often use the phrase "cultural competency" when referring to engaging difference. Cultural competence can be defined as a composite set of tailored actions, behaviors, and attitudes which enable a person or institution to function with efficacy in cross-cultural environments. (Cross, Bazron, Dennis, & Isaacs, 1989; Isaacs & Benjamin, 1991). In plain usage in the workplace, cultural competences allows for the appropriate delivery of services to all constituents and stakeholders. The word *culture* is used as it includes a person or groups' total way of life including thoughts, communications, actions, customs, beliefs, values, and institutions. The word *competence* is used because it implies having the capacity to function in a particular way: the capacity to function within the context of culturally integrated patterns of human behavior defined by a group. Being competent in cross–cultural functioning means learning new patterns of behavior and effectively applying them in the appropriate settings.

One of the challenges for institutional change, at least when it comes to diversity, is the development of personally impacting initiatives that ultimately drive institutional change. There is a diversity of opinions about diversity, and as such, making individual inroads is essential to multicultural organizational development. Day-Vines (2000) indicates that in order for systems to create truly inclusive, multicultural acceptance in the workplace, classroom, or community placement, there must be a personal commitment to "recognize, validate, and affirm" (p. 3) individuals from diverse cultures and backgrounds. Day-Vines continues with a discussion on various multicultural competencies that educators and social service professionals should possess, including a commitment to: examining personal biases; the recognition of social realities, racism, oppression, power and privilege; and learning factual knowledge about different cultures.

Each person who enters the organizational community impacts and influences the academic and social experience of others. Each of us brings a wealth of experience, heritage, values and beliefs, traditions, and customs that enrich our community in myriad ways. Every one of us is diverse; we have each experienced the world from a unique perspective that has been shaped by the intersections of gender, race, socioeconomic class, religious tradition, sexual orientation, age, geography and nationality, language, and so many more factors. The differences that we each bring to the community, then, have the potential to richly benefit the working and learning environment. These benefits can be life-long, providing the mechanisms to foster and bolster engagement across levels of difference.

Beginning with the level of personal engagement with these issues, diversity awareness programs should invite participants to become reflective about their own cultural orientations—the ways each of us has been socialized to believe and think the way we do. This reflection includes:

- **Cultural Identity Development.** We each should embark on a journey of self-discovery of our own cultural identities and how these impact our relations with others. I recommend developing a personal race, class, gender, and sexuality analysis where we acknowledge our own dominance and minority statuses.
- **Understanding My Own Cultural Complexity.** It is also important for us to recognize the ways in which we each create meaning through our own multiple identities. Each of us lives at the intersections of our cultural identities, and we need to understand this multiplicity to be truly grounded in our own selfhood.
- **Finding Common Ground.** We should stress the importance of recognizing that we all "put our pants on one leg at a time." Diversity does not build community; diversity by itself divides. Friendship and camaraderie are born out of similarity and common purpose.
- **Devilifying Majorities.** If inclusion is ever to be a reality, Whites, Males, Heterosexuals, Americans, and Christians need to be welcomed to the "diversity table." We must recognize that without allies in power groups, little change can occur.
- **Coalition Building.** The connections we make between groups of people can make or break the success of our initiatives. Let's not forget that when we work together, we learn together.

One can talk about diversity and why it is so important; the goal of professional development regarding diversity is to really understand the benefits and opportunities of a diverse education and community. For this to happen, diversity education must integrative and experiential. It is when we actively engage in long-term relationships with those who are from differing walks of life that we find out the most about ourselves—our beliefs and values—when we participate in activities that push our boundaries and limits, we find that there are multiple paths and solutions to life's challenges. Institutional priorities should include creating "global citizens" who possess vast knowledge of complex multicultural competencies. Below is a developmental process which will help trainers devise frameworks for multicultural education that minimize diversity resistance and maximize learning of diversity skills.

Stage One: Experiment

Experimental programs can be described as one-time events that are more about personal cultural awareness, cuh as ethnic dinners, cultural festivals, and special celebratory events—what Lee (1998) might terms the heroes and holidays approach.

Stage Two: Engage

Programs that engage are more academic in nature; participants learn in traditional classroom formats or the content is focused on cognitive, fact-based data and information.

Stage Three: Explore

At this more reflective level, trainers require students to be more introspective and reflective about self and society and to challenge assumptions and beliefs.

Stage Four: Experience

Programs that fit this profile require active, long term participation. These types of programs often involve intercultural teamwork and problem solving activities. Service learning and volunteer work programs often fit this type of educational offering.

By repositioning diversity education to active, experiential student learning focused on citizenship skills development, we can help prepare workers to be informed, educated leaders in society who demonstrate courage and integrity, and who have an honest commitment to addressing community problems and broader social issues through the linking and appreciation of the ideas of political astuteness, community involvement and empowerment, and social and moral responsibility to self and others. Trainers should endeavor to develop learning goals that speak to the importance of developing our workforces to be prepared to actively meet the challenges of a global marketplace. Producing citizens who can actively engage with persons from all walks of life is a primary goal of the liberal learning imperative. (Longerbeam & Sedlacek, 2006).

In order to become diverse in population and thought, multicultural in actions, beliefs, and attitudes, and inclusive in governance, curriculum development, decision-making, policy building, and community development, members of the organization must learn and be willing to critically engage each other on the issues of diversity and inclusion. Through facilitated discussion and other activities, participants can learn how to individually, departmentally, and institution develop practices that support each others' personal, social, cultural, and academic development as they engage with these important issues.

For engagement with diversity and inclusiveness to work, such engagement must be integrated into the mission, vision, and daily functions of your entire workplace or organization. There are three imperatives of diversity engagement: strategic (those individuals and organizations who are poised to navigate a global marketplace and citizenry will be ahead of the pack as population demographics shift in the next fifty years); moral (righting the wrongs of the past and protecting against future harm and under representation of disenfranchised groups); and educational (increases factual knowledge about specific group needs as well as the mechanisms for societal change). Understanding how each of these mandates impact and influence the working and learning community allows participants to build their capacities for cross-cultural engagement. Doing so allows for the development of a set of skills that help in dealing with the tensions created by diversity and for strategies in creating diversity-mature people who take personal responsibility for their attitudes and actions.

Part of being a culturally competent person is the understanding that individual identity development is impacted by interpersonal relations and societal norms. At the same time, individual identities also influence others and society. To that end, we must learn about the intersections of self and society and how understanding this plexus is important for multicultural interactions; this involves building relationships and communication with people who have divergent beliefs and values. Traditional conversations and programs about diversity are often messy, sensitive, and, for many, downright scary. How can we build effective personal relationships across (and in spite of) differences when people are afraid and unable to talk to each other? Learning outcomes for educational programs about diversity should help to expand relationship building skills by becoming more culturally self-aware, finding common ground, and by harnessing the benefits of living, working, and learning in community with others.

APPLICATION

This section highlights tried-and-true best practices gleaned from years of leading diversity initiatives. These principles have been developed from past experiences (the best and the worst) as a diversity trainer, educator, and administrator. The following strategies will assist you and your company in going to deeper levels of community engagement and cultural understanding.

Create a Common Lexicon

Most people who are inexperienced with cross-cultural engagement withdraw from these types of conversations because they are afraid of "saying the wrong thing" and thereby being labeled an –ist (racist, sexist, homophobe, etc). Those who plan diversity programs should keep in mind the importance of leveling the playing field; the more people share common definitions, the easier it will be to communicate with one another.

Later, we will highlight a set of definitions that can prove valuable for your diversity education and training programs.

Talk About the Systemic Nature of Oppression

Exclusion is encoded into the fabric of American life and society (Johnson & Blanchard, 2008); we have made major strides in civil and human rights, yet many people still are not afforded the "inalienable right to life, liberty, and the pursuit of happiness. Younger generations see footage of the terrible atrocities of slavery, the Holocaust, exclusion and internment, and believe that "things are so much better now." Yet, we live in a social system that works to the advantage of those who hold power in subtle and even unconscious ways. The unfortunate truth is that racism and other inequalities persist in 21st century America. Subtle (and not-so-subtle) manifestations of racism, classism, Anti-Semitism, heterosexism, and Ableism persist in education, employment, housing, and criminal justice. School re-segregation is occurring at alarming speeds. Some have been desensitized to the everyday examples of oppression such as name calling, telling ethnic and sexist jokes, and the use of phrases like "that's so gay." Diversity programs need to be conscious of the dynamics inherent when differing cultures interact.

Far too many people who find themselves "different" believe that their perspectives are not taken seriously; that when they speak from their own particular vantage point, they are snubbed, opinions slighted, and the complaints rage—"Oh, here we do again...why do *they* always have to talk about race (sexual orientation, etc)?" Or, "Why are they so hypersensitive?" Another common belief is the presumption that minorities were "given" their employment or scholarship because of affirmative action, but those non-minorities *earned* their way through a meritocracy.

In his book *Overcoming Our Racism: The Journey to Liberation,* Sue (2003) speaks about the pervasiveness of what he terms "micro-invalidations" and "micro-aggressions." These acts are generally innocuous and easily overlooked in a single occurrence; e.g., a person of color is asked to explain hair styles ("Can I touch your braids? It feels like Velcro or steel wool").This happening on a single occasion probably means little, but when asked for the tenth or hundredth time over a period of years, the simple and subtle become bothersome. Think of the numerous times we heard how candidate Obama was "so articulate." On the surface this comment seems complimentary except for the supposition that he was so unlike other minorities. What makes matters worse is the underlying attitudes and feelings of superiority that make the "different" seem exotic; consequently, these behaviors undermine inclusiveness, organizational harmony and efficacy, by causing feelings of being unsure, unwanted, useless in those who fail to detect and deflect them. Additionally, members of agent groups find it difficult to comprehend the sensitivity to these daily occurrences.

Focus on Issues and Principles Rather than Identity Politics

Make creating a better community the priority instead of playing the "my group" versus "your group" game of division. An example of this phenomenon is the "It's a Black thang, you wouldn't understand" that was made popular in the late 1980s. When rap and hip hop were in its fledgling stage, it was considered "black music." Those urban youth who listened to the beats began wearing t-shirts and gear reading that statement, which was meant to purposely exclude whites. The slogan became a self-fulfilling prophecy.

All models of racial, ethnic, and sexual psychosocial identity development include an immersion stage where an individual becomes grounded in their own cultural identity by surrounded only by markers of that group (Torres, Howard-Hamilton, & Cooper, 2003). This is often seen as the "pride" stage—persons wear the buttons and placards, attend the meetings and rallies, and hang out only with like-kind affinity groups.

Unfortunately, this stage also decreases one's sensitivity to the needs of other groups; what emerges is what can be called "the oppression Olympics." Immersed individuals or groups will compare whose group has had it the worst. Blacks will argue that 400 years of slavery trumps Japanese internment, while Jews decry the atrocities of the Holocaust as more significant than those who are gay and lesbian whose "sexual preferences" prohibit them from *simply* getting married. These disparate groups are so busy fighting one another; they fail to see their common enemy—oppression.

Include the "Majority" Perspective

Criticism of diversity and multiculturalism is often centered on the thought that minority groups take something that is owned by or deserving to majority groups or individuals. Persons in cultural, racial, religious, or sexual majority groups need to identify their complicity in systems of power and oppression and how unexamined dimensions of their own identities may limit their ability to effectively engage with disempowered groups. Training programs must examine the nature of dominance, including the structural and societal implications and personal dimensions of race, gender, ethnicity, nationality, language, ability, sexual orientation, religion, as well as the intersections of the above concepts. Deconstructing predominance is a mechanism to better explain the minority experience.

Persons in majority groups (see definition for in-group in chapter 3), in particular, have difficulty approaching the topics because they have been left out of the dialogue for so long. Diversity has been a predominantly minority-based discourse, and majorities feel like they are encroaching on a territory that is not their own. What we have, then, is an opportunity to demonstrate that to have a minority means to have a majority—opening the access to a dominance discourse that is so necessary in truly engaging the issues of difference. The vantage point of the majority group then becomes the authoritative context by which we come to understand socio-cultural issues.

For example, in a discussion on how race is lived in America, most conversations center on "people of color" (Blacks, Latinos, Asians, Native Americans). Whiteness, though, is the canvas upon which people of color experience life in society; they are judged for not being White. The standards of goodness and beauty in American society are White (open most beauty magazines for proof). To have a healthy and robust discussion on matters racial, whiteness must be discussed. Ignatiev (1993) suggests removing whiteness from the central core of our racialized society to allow all persons the same access and equity to resources, education, and economics—in a way, applying the same scrutiny to whiteness as has been given to the actions and attributes of minority groups for centuries.

To shine a light on whiteness is to bring to light the advantages of predominance. It also helps students understand how puritanical whiteness has been elevated in our society, mainly through the notions of ethnocentrism, the belief in the superiority of Whites, and in the argument of having "earned our way" through meritocracy (Johnson & Blanchard, 2008, p. 46).

The same is true for all agent groups: men must be included in discussion of gender; heterosexuals should understand their own sexual orientation and how heterosexuality operates in society; Christians should explore religious identity strictures; Americans must understand themselves as participants in the global society instead of the greatest superpower (and what it means to be a superpower); those from affluent financial means should seek to understand how their own socioeconomic status affects their own worldview and how they see the working class and the poor.

Value Open, Respectful Dialogue

Leave fear at the door. Good communication is at the heart of community. For many, communication is a lost art in our society. This is especially true of conversations about politics, religion, race, sexual orientation, and other points of departure. Our communication is typically one-way; we like to tell people "my opinion" but we rarely listen to one another. We have difficulty traversing cultural divides in our conversations; we even talk about cross-cultural dialogues (while we operate mostly in monologues). This is exacerbated by our two-sided coin juxtapositions; we assume only two positions (for/against, black/white, us/them, liberal/conservative) as if there are only these poles. Our adversarial positions continue to divide rather than bring together.

We prefer to "communicate" (the very term requires two-way understanding) through myopic "my way is the only way, the right way" exclusivism, or hyperbolic intellectual dishonesty, or emotional and aggressive hysteria. Rarely do we challenge ourselves and others to share balanced views of our facts (including the limitations and weaknesses of our own arguments, let alone the validity and strengths of others') (Merchant, 2008).

Having difficult dialogues is a necessity; diversity can be a "dirty word" and we need to be able to be *real* with one another in order to get beyond surface diversity issues. Establishing ground rules that honor open dialogue is essential.

Asking the Right Questions

We're all egocentric; ask questions that invite people to share their stories and heritages. Diversity conversations that focus on people's lived experiences, personal belief systems, and personal cosmologies often get to deeper levels than those centered only on data, personnel issues, and policy. We need to develop effective inquiry-based skills that empower each of us to participate fully in discussions on diversity. Inquiry skills center on a seeking of multiple explanations and information through questioning. Inquiry implies involvement that leads to understanding. Furthermore, involvement in learning implies possessing skills and attitudes that permit you to seek resolutions to questions and issues while you construct new knowledge", these become essentials to sustained and affirming diversity discussions (Heron, 1996).

Effective inquiry is more than just asking questions. Cultural competencies that have been derived from a complex inquiry method allow individuals to convert information and data into useful attitudes and behaviors—what has been called multicultural tailoring (Goldberg, 1997; Rotheram-Borus, 1993). Useful application of inquiry learning involves several factors: a context for questions, a framework for questions, a focus for questions, and different levels of questions. Designing diversity and multicultural education programs should include opportunities for critical inquiry that exposes, interrogates, and explores—holding the expectation and opportunity to substantiate opinions – without being condescending or disrespectful.

Imagine the questions that can be spurred when using clips of mainstream Hollywood films. The interdisciplinary nature of film creation, dissemination, and consumption provide great fodder for discussion. Furthermore, the cyclical nature of film's impact on the individual outlook and the societal view offers the trainer additional opportunities to engage the audience while giving lively examples of the curriculum being taught.

RAISING AWARENESS OF DIFFERENCE, POWER, AND DISCRIMINATION

Important Terms to Know

One of the most important steps to take in diversity education is to ensure that all participants in the dialogue share a common lexicon or language about diversity. Trainers who wish to explore deeper levels of diversity dialogue have a responsibility for increasing access to that dialogue. Many times individuals do not have the lexicon to participate freely; fear of "saying the wrong thing" is often very significant (especially for majority students). This reticence is a major deterrent to speaking about difference (Sparks & Singleton, 2002).

Diversity educators often talk about the necessity of cross cultural competencies; or, having the cultural awareness (of self and others), factual knowledge about the cultural traditions and mores of others, and the behavioral skills necessary to navigate cross cultural situations. In their book *Multicultural Competence in Student Affairs*, Pope, Reynolds, Mueller, and Cheatham (2004) have identified the ability to communicate across lines of difference as paramount to achieving competence. What traditional foci on differences have created are chasms that are difficult to cross. Students need to be able to have significant conversations about relationships, ethnicity, activism, and outlooks on life.

In this resource manual, we utilize the following definitions which appear in *Writing for Change: Raising Awareness of Difference, Power, and Discrimination*, a teaching kit from Teaching Tolerance, a project of the Southern Poverty Law Center (used with permission). For more information on Teaching Tolerance and its free resources for teachers and community leaders, please visit www. teachingtolerance.org.

It is important to note that the definitions below reference the systemic nature of the dynamics of difference. Teachers must assist students with establishing systemic understanding in order for them to "resist, transform, and appropriate mediated understandings, instead of passively absorbing images of who they should be and how they should act within social categorization (race, gender, class, sexual orientation, etc.)" (Jacobs, 2005, p. 7).

Anti-Semitism: systematic discrimination against, disparagement of, or oppression of Jews, Judaism, and the cultural, intellectual, and religious heritage of Jewish people.

Classism: a system of power and privilege based on the accumulation of economic wealth and social status. Classism is the mechanism by which certain groups of people, considered as a unit according to their economic, occupational, or social status, benefit at the expense of other groups.

Compulsory heterosexuality: the assumption that women are "naturally" or innately drawn sexually and emotionally toward men, and men toward women; the view that heterosexuality is the "norm" for all sexual relationships. The institutionalization of heterosexuality in all aspects of society includes the idealization of heterosexual orientation, romance, and marriage. It creates institutionalized inequality of power, and legal and social discrimination against homosexuals and the invisibility or intolerance of lesbian and gay experience.

Co-optation: various processes by which members of dominant cultures or groups assimilate members of target groups, reward them, and hold them up as models for other members of the target groups. *Tokenism* is a form of co-optation.

Difference: a characteristic that distinguishes one person from another or from an assumed "norm," or the state of being distinguished by such characteristics.

Discrimination: unequal treatment of people based on their membership in a group.

Dominance: the systematic attitudes and actions of prejudice, superiority, and self-righteousness of one group (a non-target group) in relation to another (a target group). *Internalized dominance* includes the inability of a group or individual to see privilege as a member of the non-target group.

Ethnocentrism: the emotional attitude that one's own ethnic group, nation, or culture is superior to all others or is the norm by which others are measured.

Gender: a cultural notion of what it is to be a woman or a man; a construct based on the social shaping of femininity and masculinity. It usually includes identification with males as a class or with females as a class. Gender includes subjective concepts about character traits and expected behaviors that vary from place to place and person to person.

Heterosexism: a system of beliefs, actions, advantages and assumptions in the superiority of heterosexuals and heterosexuality. It includes unrecognized privileges of heterosexual people and the exclusion of non- heterosexual people from policies, procedures, events, and decisions about what is important.

Homophobia: thoughts, feelings or actions based on fear, dislike, judgment, or hatred of gay men and lesbians/of those who love and sexually desire those of the same sex. Homophobia has roots in sexism and can include prejudice, discrimination, harassment, and acts of violence.

In-group (non-target group): the people in each system or relation of oppression who are in power in that oppression. Members of non-target groups are socialized into the role of being oppressive, becoming perpetrators or perpetuators of the cycle of oppression, either actively or indirectly. A non-target group may retain its power through force, the threat of force, and/or misinformation about the target group. Members of non-target groups also have a history of resistance that usually is not recognized.

Invisibility: the absence of target groups from the media, policies, procedures, legislation, social activities, and other milieus, which reinforces the notion, conscious or unconscious, that non-target groups are the norm. Invisibility contributes to the disempowerment of target groups and the perpetuation of the cycle of oppression.

Oppression: the systematic, institutionalized mistreatment of one group of people by another for any reason. Oppression is based on a complicated and changing network of unequal power relations.

Out-group (target group): the people in each system or relation of oppression who are without power in that oppression. Members of target groups are socialized into the role of being oppressed, internalizing the mistreatment and misinformation about the group(s) to which they belong. Each target group usually also has a history of resistance, which may not be recognized by people outside the target group.

Power: generally, the accumulation of money, goods, authority, sway, or influence. Specifically, the differential ability, based on unequal distribution of wealth, influence, or, physical force, to control the economic, political, sexual, educational, and other important decisions of others.

Prejudice: an opinion, prejudgment or attitude formed with the perception of sufficient knowledge about a group or its members.

Privilege: an invisible set of unearned rights, benefits, or assets that belong to certain individuals simply by virtue of their membership in a particular non-target group. Privilege is a dynamic system of overlapping benefits which may act to any particular individual's benefit in one set of circumstances and to that person's detriment in another.

Racism: the systematic mistreatment of people of color based on the belief in the inherent superiority of one race and thereby the right to dominance. Racism is one manifestation of institutionalized differences in economic, social, and political power in which members of some ethnic and cultural groups benefit at the expense of others.

Sexism: the systematic economic, sexual, educational, physical, and other oppression of women as a group; the exploitation and social dominance of members of one sex by another.

Social justice: a combination of laws, behaviors, and attitudes promoting equal rights and fair treatment of all members of society. The practice of social justice includes resistance to racism, sexism, classism, and other forms of oppression.

Stereotype: an exaggerated belief, image, or distorted truth about a person or group—a generalization that allows for little or no individual differences or social variation.

Please note that these definitions often refer to the "isms" as systemic and institutional. This is an important part of the education of difference. Bigotry and bias are indeed personal and individual, but their greatest impact is at the societal level. Encourage your participants to learn these definitions as a part of the central curriculum. The film clips used later in this resource manual will be based upon these definitions.

With each clip you will find the topical definition being highlighted, a plot summary of the entire movie, a description of the featured clip, and information related to the time to start and stop the scene on a DVD (scene or chapter is marked as well). Please note that the elapsed times can vary by machine by a few seconds; this is where the scene descriptions become helpful. Some of the clips are representative of more than one definition; some films have more than one highlighted clip. Below is an example of the treatment of the included film clips.

[Title of film]	[Highlighted Definition(s)]
Higher Learning	**SEXISM/DISCRIMINATION**

[Description of film]

Director John Singleton weaves an interlocking tale of the struggles of freshman year at fictional Columbus University—dealing with diversity, identity, and belonging. Malik (Omar Epps) is a new student at Columbus and he is quickly overwhelmed by the collegiate life. He and his roommate are from differing backgrounds, his professor (Laurence Fishburne) rides him, and race relations are at an all-time low.

[Description of highlighted scene]

Kristen (Kristy Swanson) is passing out flyers for Students for a Non-Sexist Society, a women's group that discusses issues of sexuality and safety and security. A male named Wayne asks Kristen for a flyer, but she refuses and says that the group is only open to women; Wayne challenges this as contradictory: "You want a non-sexist society, but you won't give me a flyer because I'm a man? That's not cool." Kristen wonders, "Well, why do you really want to come?" The scene ends as Wayne compliments her new hair style.

[Film details]

Elapsed time: This scene begins at 01:05:00 and ends at 01:05:54 (DVD Scene 13)
Rating: R for sexual violence and strong language
Citation: *Higher Learning* (Columbia Pictures, 1994), written and directed by John Singleton

While they may, the clips offered here are not designed to offer commentary or criticism about the overall film itself, nor of the actors, directors, or writers, or the film industry, but to complement the educational objectives of the training session. Participants (or yourself as the trainer) may, however, desire to offer critique after viewing selected scenes; this may provoke additional fruitful discussion about the creation and maintenance of systems of power and discrimination which exist in our society.

Most of the clips in this resource manual last less than ten minutes; there may be a few exceptions. It is highly recommended that the trainer or facilitator set the context for the participants by briefly introducing the plot of the film, the action in the selected scene, what they should be watching for (specific characters' activities, discussion exchanges, particular language, etc.). Doing this helps to minimize the entertainment factor of the movie clip, and asks the participant to become actively engaged and critically thinking about the purpose of using the film.

Trainers are strongly encouraged to preview any clips prior to showing them to an audience. Some of the clips in this manual include strong language, profanity, nudity, and mature themes. It is up to the trainer to decide what is developmentally, socially, and professionally appropriate for the audience. If you do not preview a clip, you are asking for embarrassment and in extreme cases, the loss of your job.

A Note about Using Film Clips

Mainstream Hollywood moving images have, since the advent of the silent movies, have changed that way we see and think about ourselves and others. While many believe that film is all about entertainment, educational research touts the validity of film as an educational tool. For educators and trainers who use film, the most significant barrier, however, is the time factor. Using film clips allows trainers to harness the film medium and make it useful to enhance the goals of the educational program. Using mainstream film clips, whether historical or contemporary, can make training materials more relevant, engaging, and active. Additionally, by using clips, the trainer who talks using themes or materials from Hollywood, does not lose someone who may not have seen the entire film. This provides an immediate and common ground for all participants—that is actually a fun way of getting your participants connected with one another and the material at the center of discussion.

Whenever possible, play clips with the subtitles on; engaging the brain on multiple levels enhances understanding. You may hear complaints from participants who see the captions as cumbersome and "in the way," but here is a great way of modeling inclusivity of those who may have hearing challenges.

A Note about Copyright

Film clips, however short, are protected by U.S. copyright laws (Title 17); permission to show copyrighted films is required by law. Many trainers operate under *fair use* regulations for educators. Fair use allows for limitations of the exclusive rights of copyright owners. The United States Copyright Office outlines the following guidelines for using movies for educational purposes:

It is not necessary to obtain permission if you show the movie in the course of "face-to-face teaching activities" in a nonprofit educational institution, in a classroom or similar place devoted to instruction, if the copy of the movie being performed is a lawful copy. 17 U.S.C. § 110(1). This exemption encompasses instructional activities relating to a wide variety of subjects, but it does not include performances for recreation or entertainment purposes, even if there is cultural value or intellectual appeal. (http://www.copyright.gov/help/faq/faq-fairuse.html)

Please consult your parent organization's policy on fair use and other copyright permissions before showing any of the clips detailed here. [The film descriptions are written with enough detail that showing the clips is not necessary—although strongly recommended).

FILM CLIPS

21   **PRIVILEGE**

Trained by their teacher, five MIT wunderkinds learn to use their smarts for personal gain by counting cards in Las Vegas casinos. Ben Campbell joins the group with the hopes of winning enough money to pay for an Ivy League education at Harvard. Based on a true story.

Ben Campbell (Jim Sturgess) is walking with his teacher and mentor, Professor Micky Rosa (Kevin Spacey) while Rosa tries to convince Ben to join his squad of secret card counters who make big money at the casinos playing blackjack. Rosa wants Ben to be his star player because he doesn't trust the others; Ben, an intelligent student from MIT, is not sure. Micky flatters Ben by saying that Ben is much like he used to be. Ben agrees to join the team, and Rosa tells him to get ready for the trip the next day. Ben complains that he has a quantitative literacy exam the next day, but Micky tells him that he has already talked to the professor saying that Ben was working on a special assignment and had already earned an A for the exam. Before he walks away, Micky turns and says, "You see, Ben, amazing things can happen from the inside."

Elapsed time: This scene begins at 00:36:07 and ends at 00:37:42 (DVD Scene 10)
Rating: PG-13 for some violence, and sexual content including partial nudity
Citation: *21* (Columbia Pictures, 2008) screenplay written by Peter Steinfeld & Allan Loeb, directed by Robert Luketic

300   **ETHNOCENTRISM**

Based on Frank Miller's graphic novel, the action follows King Leonidas and his brave group of 300 Spartan soldiers as they prepare to defend their native Greece from the invasion of King Xerxes of Persia. As the small army fights, Leonidas' wife fights for him within the council, but her plans are foiled by a duplicitous senator.

Dilio, the story's narrator, begins telling the story of how Leonidas had become the king of ancient Sparta. He tells the people that a great army of soldiers (what he called a "beast") was heading towards "sacred Sparta" to devour it be war. The emissary from Persia greets King Leonidas and asks him to surrender peacefully to the Persian king, Xerxes. The queen responds to the messenger, "Don't be coy or stupid Persian. You can afford neither in Sparta." The messenger retorts, "What makes this woman think she can speak among men?" The queen responds, "Because only Spartan women give birth to real men." Leonidas refuses the route of submission to Xerxes and mentions other Grecian communities who have also denied Xerxes' request. He states, "Rumor has it, the Athenians have already turned you down; and if those philosophers and boy-lovers have found that kind of nerve…; Spartans have their reputation to consider." The scene ends when Leonidas screams "This is Sparta" and kicks the emissary down an artesian well.

Elapsed time: This scene begins at 00:05:15 and ends at 00:44:06 (DVD Scene 2)
Rating: R for graphic battle sequences throughout, some sexuality and nudity
Citation: *300* (Warner Bros. Pictures, 2007) screenplay written by Zack Snyder, Kurt Johnstad, & Michael Gordon, directed by Zack Snyder

300   **DISCRIMINATION/OUT GROUP**
Based on Frank Miller's graphic novel, the action follows King Leonidas and his brave group of 300 Spartan soldiers as they prepare to defend their native Greece from the invasion of King Xerxes of Persia. As the small army fights, Leonidas' wife fights for him within the council, but her plans are foiled by a duplicitous senator.

Leonidas and his general are discussing a plan to cut off their enemies' access to the city when a hunch-backed soldier named Ephialtes offers his services to his king. The general refers to Ephialtes as a "monster" and keeps him at bay with his sword. Leonidas notices Ephialtes' Spartan cloak and Ephialtes describes how he came to live outside of the city walls. He mentions, "My mother's love led my parents to flee Sparta lest I be discarded." Ephialtes humbly requests to join the combat in order to redeem his father's name. "My father trained me to feel no fear", Ephialtes says, "to make spear and shield and sword as a much a part of me as my own beating heart." Ephialtes' deformity limits his ability to raise his shield, and Leonidas rejects his request to serve citing "Not all of us were made to be soldiers." He continues, "If you want to help in a Spartan victory, clear the battlefield of the dead, tend the wounded, bring them water, but as for the fight itself, I cannot use you." The scene ends as Leonidas walks away leaving Ephialtes screaming to the wind, "Mother, Father—you were wrong! Leonidas, you are wrong."

Elapsed time: This scene begins at and ends at (DVD Scene 13)
Rating: R for graphic battle sequences throughout, some sexuality and nudity
Citation: *300* (Warner Bros. Pictures, 2007) screenplay written by Zack Snyder, Kurt Johnstad, & Michael Gordon, directed by Zack Snyder

Ace Ventura, Pet Detective   **HOMOPHOBIA**
Hired to find Snowflake the dolphin, the missing mascot of the Miami Dolphins, Ace Ventura stumbles upon a conspiracy involving a disgraced football player and the police force. Let the hilarity ensue as Jim Carrey leads this comedic masterpiece.

Ace (Jim Carrey) has been struggling to solve the case of a missing dolphin; his biggest obstacle is drawing connections between Ray Finkle, a missing placekicker for the Miami Dolphins, and Lois Einhorn, the female chief of the local police department. Ordinarily, Ace has warmness towards all animals, but his own pets are facing his frustrated ire. His puppy wants food, but Ace shoos him away. When the dog lies down on the cover of a magazine with Finkle's picture on it, Ace figures out that Einhorn is actually Finkle in disguise. As he makes the realization, Ace panics as he remembers that earlier in the day, he and Einhorn had shared a passionate kiss. He shrieks, "Oh my God, Einhorn is a man" and his face grimaces with disgust, and Ace sprints to the bathroom and pukes violently, frantically brushes his teeth, even going as far as using a plunger on his face to force himself to vomit more. He removes all of his clothing, sets them on fire in a trash can, and jumps into the shower repeatedly crying "no" in a mournful manner as the scene closes.

Elapsed time: This scene begins at 01:06:30 and ends at 01:08:40 (DVD Scene 24)
Rating: PG-13 for off-color humor and some nudity
Citation: *Ace Ventura, Pet Detective* (Warner Bros. Pictures, 1994) written by Jack Bernstein, directed by Tom Shadyac

Alvin and the Chipmunks   **CO-OPTATION**
The classic children's trio of singing rodents comes to life in this family adventure. Alvin, Simon, and Theodore are adopted by Dave Seville, a struggling songwriter, who quickly turns them into the latest pop music sensation. Ian Hawke (Dave Cross) plays a record executive who will stop at nothing to have the chipmunks all to himself.

Alvin, Simon, and Theodore, three talking chipmunks, are trying to revive Dave Seville, whose home the chipmunks have invaded. Dave had passed out from the surprise of talking animals. When he awakens, Dave acknowledges, "Chipmunks can't talk." He questions if all animals have the ability to talk. Alvin asks, "Do all humans have houses that smell like sweat socks?" The trio officially introduce themselves to Dave and he responds, "Nice to meet you. Now get out of my house!" "But we talk," one of the boys states. Dave responds, "Which only makes me want you out of my house that much more. It's creepy, unnatural, somewhat evil." Dave captures the three under a bowl and throws them outside. Later, the chipmunks are singing outside in perfect harmony and Dave overhears them and is shocked at their ability to sing. Hearing them, Dave invites them back into the house. He offers them a deal for being able to stay inside—"You guys sing my songs, you get to sleep here." He stipulates that they are not permitted to let their animal friends "because I don't want to come home and find a bunch of rabbits and skunks on my couch." Simon refers to Dave as their only friend, but Dave says, "Let's not get ahead of ourselves here. Let's just start with me being your songwriter." The scene ends after the boys discuss their Christmas plans and Dave tucks them in for the night—"We start work tomorrow. I want you bright eyed and bushy tailed by 8:00." Alvin states, "My tail is not bushy until 9:00," to which Dave responds, "Not my problem. Go to sleep."

Elapsed time: This scene begins at 00:14:11 and ends at 00:20:50 (DVD Scene 6)
Rating: PG for mild, rude humor

Citation: *Alvin & the Chipmunks* (Fox 2000 Pictures, 2007) screenplay written by John Vitti, Will McRobb, & Chris Viscardi, directed by Tim Hill

American Beauty   **HOMOPHOBIA**
Struggling to come to grips with his own midlife crisis, Lester Burnham (Kevin Spacey) seeks to redefine his role as husband and father after falling for his daughter's best friend, Angela (Mena Suvari).

The Fitts family has recently moved into a new home, and on this particular morning, the family is having breakfast when they hear a knock on the door. Colonel Frank Fitts opens the door and is greeted by Jim Olymer (Scott Bakula) and Jim Berkeley (Sam Robards), who identify themselves as "partners" who live next door and are bringing them a welcome-to-the-neighborhood basket of treats from the garden. Colonel Fitts (Chris Cooper) asks what type of business the partners are involved in; one is an attorney, the other is an anesthesiologist. The scene flashes to Colonel Fitts and his son Ricky (Wes Bentley) are riding in a car. Frank questions "How come these faggots always have to rub it in your face? How can they be so shameless?" Ricky responds, "That's the whole thing, Dad. They don't feel that's anything to be ashamed of." Frank returns, "Well it is." Ricky mechanically speaks to his father (a Marine), "Forgive me, sir, for speaking so bluntly, but those fags make me want to puke my fucking guts out." Seemingly pleased with his son's answer, Frank responds, "Well, me too, son. Yeah, me too."

Elapsed time: This scene begins at 00:23:50 and ends at 00:26:23 (DVD Scene 6)
Rating: R for strong sexuality, language, violence and drug content
Citation: *American Beauty* (Dreamworks SKG, 1999) written by Alan Ball, directed by Sam Mendes

American History X   **ETHNOCENTRISM/RACISM**
Derek Vinyard (Ed Norton) has spent most of his life as a leader of a Neo-Nazi skinhead group; he has even done time in prison for a violent attack on several men. When he learns that his young brother is following down the same path, Derek turns over a new leaf and tries to get his brother to mend the error of his ways.

The captain of the police force has assembled a team of officers to discuss the proliferation of white supremacist gang activity in the Venice Beach area. They are joined by Dr. Bob Sweeney, the principal of the local high school who does outreach work in the local community. The team begins to discuss the gang history of Derek Vinyard, who is leader of the skinhead sect who has been released from jail that morning. They also discuss Cameron Alexander, who is Derek's mentor and protégé. The captain acknowledges "There were no white gangs in Venice Beach before Cameron Alexander and Derek Vinyard hooked up." In describing Vinyard's "baggage," the captain inserts a news report about the murder of Derek's father who was a firefighter gunned down while putting out a fire at a supposed drug dealer's home. Derek describes his feelings about the changing demographics in the town: "Well, this country's becoming a haven for criminals, so what do you expect? You know, decent, hard working Americans like my dad are getting rubbed out by social parasites—blacks, browns, yellow, whatever." The reporter asks Derek if he believes his father's murder was race related; Derek responds, "Yeah, it's race related. Every problem in this country is race related—not just crime—it's immigration, AIDS, welfare—those are problems of the black community, the Hispanic community, the Asian community; they're not white problems. They're not products of their environments. Minorities don't give two shits about this country. They come here to exploit it, not embrace it. Millions of white European Americans came here and flourished within a generation. What the fuck is the matter with these people? They have to go around shooting at firemen." The reporter asks what is the significance of his tirade and Derek responds, "Because my father was murdered doing his job—putting out a fire in a fucking nigger neighborhood he shouldn't even have given a shit about. He got shot by a fucking drug dealer who probably still collects a welfare check. The scene ends when the captain and Dr. Sweeney suggest keeping an eye on Derek.

Elapsed time: This scene begins at 00:12:10 and ends at 00:16:00 (DVD Scene 5)
Rating: R for graphic brutal violence including rape, pervasive language, strong sexuality and nudity
Citation: *American History X* (New Line Cinema, 1998) written by David McKenna, directed by Tony Kaye

Anchorman: The Legend of Ron Burgundy   SEXISM

It's the 1970's as San Diego anchorman Ron Burgundy (Will Farrell) is the top dog in network TV, which gives way to his freewheeling sexism with his fraternal-like crew. But all that's about to change (or be jeopardized) when ambitious reporter Veronica Corningstone (Christina Applegate) has just arrived as a new employee at his TV station.

The station manager, Mr. Harken (Fred Willard), is introducing a new member of the news team, Miss Veronica Corningstone (Christina Applegate). The scene breaks to witness Brian Fantana (Paul Rudd) and several others complaining to Mr. Harken. Fantana argues, "I mean, come on Ed, it's bull crap. Don't get me wrong, I love the ladies! I mean, they rev my engine, but they don't belong in the newsroom. Champ Kind (David Koechner) breaks in, "It is anchorman, not anchor lady! And that is a scientific fact!" Ron adds, "It's terrible. She has beautiful eyes and her hair smells like cinnamon!" Mr. Harken reassures that she will not be taking anyone's air time. Brick Tamland (Steve Carrell) rants "I read somewhere that their periods attract bears. Bears can smell their menstruation." Because of this, Brian argues having a woman around will put "the whole station in jeopardy." Champ defends, "I will say one thing for her, Ed; she does have a nice, big old behind. I'd like to put some barbecue sauce on that butt and just bite, bite, bite, munch, munch, munch" and makes a series of lewd gestures. Veronica enters the room to ask when her office would be ready; Harken tells her it will take a while. When Veronica leaves, the catcalls continue; Champ picks up where he left off: "Oh she is one saucy mama!" Outside, Corningstone overhears and as she walks towards the newsroom, she thinks, "Here we go again. Every station it's the same. Women ask me how I put up with it. Well, the truth is, I don't really have a choice. This is definitely a man's world; but while they're laughing and grab-assing, I'm chasing down leads and practicing my non-regional diction. Because the only way to win is to be the best—the very best." The scene ends when Veronica sits on the desk.

Elapsed time: This scene begins at 00:14:45 and ends at 00:17:28 (DVD Scene 5)
Rating: PG-13 for sexual humor, language and comic violence
Citation: *Anchorman: the Legend of Ron Burgundy* (DreamWorks, 2004), written by Will Ferrell & Adam McKay, directed by Adam McKay

The Ant Bully   IN-GROUP
Lucas Nickle is tired of being picked on by the local bullies, and he takes his frustrations out on the ant colony is his backyard. He floods the anthill with his squirt gun and a hose, and he stomps on the fleeing ants. To get revenge, Zoc the ant wizard creates a potion that shrinks Lucas to ant-size. Lucas is forced into hard labor in the colony, but soon becomes a hero when he saves the ants from certain demise when the exterminator is called.

As the scene opens, a group of ants are collecting food to carry back to the colony when they overhear a group of humans screaming "Dogpile!" Soon a human falls to the ground and the ants point to him and yell, "Destroyer" and run away. The boy, Lucas Nickle, is being given an "atomic wedgy" by the neighborhood bully. Lucas complains that he is running out of underwear, but the bully responds, "What are you going to do about it, huh? Nothing. Because I'm big and you're small." The bully and his friends walk away, leaving Lucas alone to pick up his squirt gun. With a menacing look on his face, Lucas heads over to a large anthill where he sees the ants entering the colony. Lucas begins spraying the anthill with large bursts from his water pistol, which sends thousands of ants scrambling for safety. Towering over the defenseless ants, Lucas repeats what the bully had said to him—"What you going to do about it, ants? Nothing. Because I'm big and you're small." Lucas tosses the plastic gun and kicks the anthill sending ants flying through the air. He then tries to smash the ants with his shoe. The scene ends when Lucas' mother calls him to come home.

Elapsed time: This scene begins at 00:02:47 and ends at 00:05:52 (DVD Scene 2)
Rating: PG for mild rude humor and action
Citation: *The Ant Bully* (Warner Bros. Pictures, 2006) written for the screen and directed by John A. Davis

As Good as It Gets   HOMOPHOBIA
Melvin Udall (Jack Nicholson), a cantankerous, reclusive curmudgeon with little social skills, falls in love with Carol Connelly (Helen Hunt), a single mother of a sickly child. Carol finds a way to tame the savage beast raging within the obsessive compulsive Udall.

Melvin (Jack Nicholson) is in his apartment working on his latest novel when he is interrupted by his neighbor Simon (Greg Kinnear). Melvin is as rude as they come and as when he answers the door, he begins to hurl slurs at Simon, who is gay. Melvin roars, "Son of a bitch! Pansy ass stool pusher!" Simon is afraid of Melvin and begins to back away, but decides to engage and tells Melvin that he had found his missing dog (which Melvin had thrown in the garbage chute in a previous scene). Melvin chides Simon for interrupting him while he is working, indicating that Simon should never knock on his door again. Melvin asks, "Do you like to be interrupted when you're nancing around your garden?" He does not want to be interrupted "even if there's a fire. Not even if you hear the sound of a thud from my home and one week later there is the smell coming from there that can only be a decaying human body and you have to hold a hanky to your face because the stench is so thick you think you're gonna faint. Even then don't come knocking. Or if it's election night, and you're excited and you want to celebrate because some fudge packer you date has been elected the first queer president of the United States and he's going to have you down to Camp David and you want someone to share the moment with. Even then, don't knock, not on this door, not for any reason. Do you get me, sweetheart?" Simon responds, "Yes. It's not a subtle point you're making." The scene ends when Melvin closes the door in Simon's face.

Elapsed time: This scene begins at 00:05:47 and ends at 00:08:30 (DVD Scene 2)
Rating: PG 13 for appeal for strong language, thematic elements, nudity and a beating
Citation: *As Good as It Gets* (TriStar Pictures, 1997) written by Mark Andrus & James Brooks, directed by James Brooks

Beauty Shop   STEREOTYPE/GENDER

Gina Norris has always had a dream of owning her own beauty salon, and has been frustrated by working for the likes of Jorge (Kevin Bacon). When Jorge starts making her take care of his clients, Gina quits and branches out on her own (and takes many of Jorge's clients with her). Her new shop, set in an urban area in Atlanta, is a far cry from her posh clientele with Jorge, who will stop at nothing to see Gina fail.

Gina Norris (Queen Latifah) has just opened her new beauty salon, and on this day the inspector from the state boards gives her a citation for having left piles of equipment in the alley behind the store. Gina tried to explain that movers were coming to haul the material away, but the inspector fined her anyway. Moments later, the moving truck arrives and a very handsome, muscular young man emerges from the driver's side. Gina and her fellow female hairdressers are ogling the young man. Gina is also impressed by the cornrow-style braiding in the man's hair and questions where he has his hair styled. When James admits that he does his own hair, Gina hires him as a stylist for the salon, despite his just being released from prison. James becomes an instant fan favorite of the female clientele; his fellow stylists, however, question his sexual orientation. Chantel (Golden Brooks), Ida (Sherri Shepherd), and Lynn (Alicia Silverstone) are discussing James' looks and appearance: "But I'm telling you; something just ain't right," Chantel argues. "It's like he's too good looking," returns Ida. Ms. Josephine (Alfre Woodard) chimes in, "You can't tell by looking at the brother if he's gender specific." Ida interrupts, "Josephine, come on! Look at the muscles on that boy. Fifty percent pumping iron; the rest from fightin' brothers off that booty." Chantel adds, "He got a little swish down river." Lynn stands on her convictions that he is heterosexual. Their "proof" comes when Gina serves James a cup of cappuccino and James drinks with his pinky finger in the air. Chantel flails her hand in the air and states, "Swish, swish." The scene ends as three ladies begin dancing flamboyantly quoting lines from a RuPaul song popular in the drag queen community.

Elapsed time: This scene begins at 00:44:42 and ends at 00:49:08 (DVD Scene 10)
Rating: PG-13 for sexual material, language and brief drug references
Citation: *Beauty Shop* (Metro Goldwyn Mayer, 2005), screenplay written by Kate Lanier & Norman Vance, directed by Billie Woodruff

The Bee Movie   **OPPRESSION**
Imagine a world where bees and humans have conversations with one another. Barry Benson is dissatisfied with life in the hive and branches out to see how the other half lives. When he learns that bees are being duped into producing honey for human commercialism, he sets on a course that goes all the way to court. For the first time in history, man and insect duke it out in the court of law.

Barry B. Benson (voiced by Jerry Seinfeld) has left his hive to explore the human world where he becomes fast friends with a human named Vanessa Bloome (Renee Zelwegger). Vanessa and Barry are walking down the street asking each other questions; Barry continually gets swatted at by passersby. When they enter the grocery store, a stock boy swats Barry with a rolled newspaper. Just then, Barry notices the numerous jars of honey on the shelves and is disturbed by what he perceives as exploitation at the hands of human beings. He follows a truck to Honey Farms where he sees hundred of makeshift hives; two beekeepers are talking about the honey collection process when one unveils a new smoker (used to anesthetize the bees for collection) that gives the bees "twice the nicotine, *all* the tar." One beekeeper mentions how they profit from the bees' work—"We throw it [the honey] in jars, slap a label on it and it's pretty much pure profit. They make the honey; we make the money." They refer to the bees as "having brains the size of pinheads." Back at his home hive, Barry tries to explain his plans to undo the exploitative practices. "I want to do this for all our lives," Barry says, "nobody works harder than bees." He describes how bees survive on only two cups of honey per year while human beings use the honey in cosmetics and other frivolities. The scene ends when Barry's dad asks him, "What can one bee do?"

Elapsed time: This scene begins at 00:31:35 and ends at 00:41:32 (DVD Scene 7)
Rating: PG for mild suggestive humor
Citation: *The Bee Movie* (Dreamworks Animation, 2007) written by Jerry Seinfeld, Spike Fersten, Barry Marder, & Andy Robin, directed by Simon Smith & Steve Hickner

The Bee Movie   IN-GROUP/OUT-GROUP

Imagine a world where bees and humans have conversations with one another. Barry Benson is dissatisfied with life in the hive and branches out to see how the other half lives. When he learns that bees are being duped into producing honey for human commercialism, he sets on a course that goes all the way to court. For the first time in history, man and insect duke it out in the court of law.

Barry B. Benson (voiced by Jerry Seinfeld) has chosen to take his fight against the honey industry to court. In the opening statement, the honey companies' lawyer, Mr. Montgomery, describes the natural order of human dominance in the world. He refers to "man's divine right to benefit from the bounty of nature God put before us." [He has already stepped on a bug on his way into the courtroom and held up a honey packet and sarcastically asked if Barry had worked on its production]. He scoffs at the idea of having to "negotiate with a silkworm for the elastic in my britches." He attempts to capitalize on the fears of the jury by suggesting that Barry (a talking bee) is some Hollywood trick or some governmental conspiracy. Barry responds that he is just an ordinary bee and describes the importance of honey to bee life—"We invented it. We make it, and we protect it with our lives. Unfortunately there are some people in this room who think they can take whatever they want from us because we're the little guys." He continues, "I'm hoping that after all this is over, you'll see by taking our honey, you're not only taking away everything we have, but everything we are." Each side begins to call witnesses. Barry calls Mr. Klauss Vanderhayden, the head of the major honey companies (Honey Farms, Honeyburton, and Honron) who hires the beekeepers. Barry asks if there are any "bee freers" on these farms and questions the appropriateness of using the image of a bear on honey jars ("Bears kill bees!"). Barry then calls rock legend Sting to the stand where he grills him on the appropriation of his stage name—"Here we have yet another example of bee culture casually stolen by a human for nothing more than a prance-about stage name." Actor Ray Liotta is also called to the stand as the spokesperson for "Ray Liotta's Private Select Honey." Pointing at Liotta, Barry says "This isn't a goodfella. This is a badfella." Liotta responds by trying to hit Barry with his Emmy award; Liotta questions, "Why doesn't someone just step on this little creep, and we can all go home?"

Elapsed time: This scene begins at 00:44:58 and ends at 00:50:45 (DVD Scene 9)
Rating: PG for mild suggestive humor
Citation: *The Bee Movie* (Dreamworks Animation, 2007) written by Jerry Seinfeld, Spike Fersten, Barry Marder, & Andy Robin, directed by Simon Smith & Steve Hickner

Be Kind Rewind   HOMOPHOBIA

Intent of making a documentary of the life legendary jazz musician Fats Waller, Mike (Mos Def) works at a video store to earn money. When his friend becomes a human magnet and erases the entire collection of videos, Mike and Jerry (Jack Black) remake each film—starring themselves.

Jerry (Jack Black) and Mike (Mos Def) must recreate the action of the film *Rush Hour 2* for a customer who threatens to take his business to a larger franchise. They are working with several other "actors" from the neighborhood, including Wilson (Irv Gooch), the mechanic who is playing the female lead role (even though he is a male). In one of the scenes, Jerry, who is playing the Jackie Chan character, holds a bomb in his mouth and must kiss Wilson who holds the detonator. Jerry is clearly uncomfortable and whispers to Mike, "I don't want to kiss Wilson!" Overhearing this, Wilson quits the movie and walks off the set. Jerry continues to complain: "Maybe you can understand I don't want the whole neighborhood to think I'm having a homosexual interracial relationship with my mechanic?" Mike questions if the interracial aspect is really the problem, and Jerry counteracts, "Forget about the interracial thing, but kissing my mechanic is disturbing and inappropriate; he could sue me for sexual harassment." The scene ends as Jerry declares that he has a better idea.

Elapsed time: This scene begins at 00:37:55 and ends at 00:41:03 (DVD Scene 8)
Rating: PG-13 for some sexual references
Citation: *Be Kind Rewind* (New Line Cinema, 2008) written and directed by Michel Gondry

Benchwarmers   **DISCRIMINATION/OUT-GROUP**
Three grown men with a childhood chip on their shoulders decide to challenge take on all little league challengers in three-man baseball. They become the champions for all wannabes and social outcasts.

Three socially inept young children are playing baseball in the local park when members of the organized little league team try to force them off the diamond. One of the young kids argues that the team's practice does not start until 4:30; the team leader states "We want to have a practice before the practice." A girl who was with the original group suggests they all play together when an older boy retorts "No, because you suck. Why don't you go home and build your science projects." The oldest boy pushes the other boy down, and while another team member holds him, the oldest nearly sits on the boy's face and gives him some "beef stew" (he farted just above his nose). The young boy is rescued when an adult (played by Ron Schneider) chases the older boys away. In tears, the young boy tells the adult, "It actually didn't taste as bad as you'd think" and runs away.

Elapsed time: This scene begins at 00:00:50 and ends at 00:04:04 (DVD Scene 1)
Rating: PG-13 for language and sexual
Citation: *Benchwarmers* (Revolution Studios, 2006) written by Allen Covert & Nick Swardson, directed by Dennis Dugan

Beverly Hills Chihuahua   **DISCRIMINATION/CLASSISM**
A pampered pooch manages to get separated from her owner while on vacation in Mexico. Used to living in the lap of luxury, Chloe must brave the streets and slums while befriending the local dogs and learning to see how the other half lives.

Chloe (voiced by Drew Barrymore) is a spoiled lapdog who has just been rescued from a Mexican dog fighting ring by a German Shepherd named Delgado. Chloe asks to be taken to the Carthay Hotel, a fancy hotel where her owner is a frequent customer. Chloe and Delgado are dirty after having run through the mud; Chloe is unaware of her disheveled state. When they arrive at the Carthay, Delgado announces, "OK, here you are, your highness." Chloe cheers, "I feel like I'm home already!" As she prepares to enter the hotel, Chloe turns to Delgado and says, "Maybe you should wait out here. [pause] I don't mean it like it sounds, but they can be a little particular about the dogs they let in." The front desk clerk is trying to shoo her away when two other pampered pooches enter the lobby of the hotel. One of the dogs bumps into Chloe and exclaims, "Eww, it touched me!" The other bellows "Get this mutt out of here!" Chloe declares, "Mutt! I have been a preferred customer at this hotel for years." Chloe is ejected from the hotel and when the door closes, she sees her reflection in a mirror and shrieks, "Oh no, I'm hideous!"

Elapsed time: This scene begins at 00:29:18 and ends at 00:30:45 (DVD Scene 4)
Rating: PG for some mild thematic elements
Citation: *Beverly Hills Chihuahua* (Art in Motion, 2008), written by Analisa LaBianco & Jeffrey Bushell, directed by Raja Gosnell

Billy Elliot   GENDER
The youngest son of a striking factory worker, Billy finds a mentor in the most unlikely of places—in a dance studio. Billy's father wants him to be a real man and signs him up for boxing lessons, but Billy has his heart set on becoming a dancer.

Billy has been taking ballet lessons (unbeknownst to his father who believes Billy has been attending boxing classes). Billy's dad has very traditional views and values; he is a striking laborer who is protesting outside of his factory with the other workers. This mayhem is contrasted with Billy's ballet class, where he is the only male student. In order to keep up the charade, Billy hides his ballet slippers in shorts and wraps boxing gloves around his neck when he leaves the house. One day his father learns of his ongoing ruse and goes to the ballet school where he is shocked to see his son dancing with all-girl squad. He orders Billy out of the class. At home later, Billy's dad is scolding him for being in the ballet. When Billy questions why ballet is bad, Billy's grandmother mentions that she used to love the ballet. In response, Billy's dad admits that it is "perfectly normal" for Nana to go to the ballet, "for girls, not for lads Billy. Lads do football or boxing or wrestling. Not friggin' ballet!" Billy continues to question why Dad feels ballet is so wrong, and the dad keeps responding "You know why." When Billy continues to push the issue, Dad threatens him with corporal punishment. Assuming that his dad believed that only gay men do ballet, Billy mentions, "It's not just poofs, Dad. Some ballet dancers are as fit as athletes." Billy is forced to quit the ballet to stay home and look after his aging grandmother. The scene after Billy and his dad get into a scrape and Billy runs from the house.

35

Elapsed time: This scene begins at 00:22:48 and ends at 00:29:18 (DVD Scene 5)
Rating: PG 13 for some thematic material
Citation: *Billy Elliot* (Working Title Films, 2000), written by Lee Hall, directed by Stephen Daldry

**The Birdcage   COMPULSORY HETEROSEXUALITY/HETEROSEXISM/
OUT-GROUP**

In an adaptation of La Cage Aux Folles, *a gay cabaret owner and his drag queen companion agree to put up a false straight front so that their son can introduce them to his fiancé's right-wing moralistic parents.*

In a previous scene, we learn that Val is the product of a one-night affair between Armand and his former co-worker, Katherine. Armand goes to see her to ask her to stand-in as Armand's wife when the Keelies come; she agrees. Unbeknownst to Armand, Albert has plans to introduce himself as "Mrs. Coleman" and this scene begins with Albert entering the room. "Mrs. Coleman" and Senator Keely make fast friends and are conversing about shared political ideals. The senator refers to the Colemans as "our kind of people" who espouse good American values as their conversation covers gender roles, gays in the military, and school prayer. The scene ends when Armand drops the ice bucket.

Elapsed time: This scene begins at 01:24:17 and ends at 01:28:48 (DVD Scene 19)
Rating: R for language
Citation: *The Birdcage* (United Artists, 1999), screenplay written by Elaine May, directed by Mike Nichols

Black Knight   SEXISM
Jamal (Martin Lawrence) works at a medieval theme park; after falling into the moat, he is magically transported to a 14th century land. He meets Victoria (Marsha Thomason), a handmaiden who is a part of a plot to overthrow the tyrannical king who has usurped the thrown from the rightful monarch.

Victoria the chambermaid is serving the men at the camp and attempts to discuss plans for relocating the group. As she is serving him, one of the men in the camp scoffs, "Interesting suggestion. And here's another interesting suggestion—serve more gruel [the other men cackle]." Jamal (Martin Lawrence) enters and chastises the men for their callous treatment of the lady. The two walk away and Jamal thanks Victoria for helping Sir Nolte [in a previous scene] save his life. Victoria offers, "Actually the plan was all mine." Jamal answers, "No shit?" Victoria adds, "I shit you not, but I had to tell everyone it was something I heard from a great warrior, otherwise no one would have listened to me—a woman." Jamal begins, "So you like me a little more than you…" but Victoria interrupts with questions about Jamal's tryst with the princess. Later, Jamal offers to take Victoria to a place "where smart women like you can do more than just ladle gruel. Look, if you show me how to get to the lake, tomorrow you'll be at Fox Hills Mall getting your legs waxed, drinking mai-tais chillin'. So, what's it going to be—gruel, leprosy, mean ass king or mai-tais, chillin', bikini, thong?" She responds, "I realize our little backwards society is far from perfect, but it's a step in the right direction. Now is the eve of our great offensive. I can live with losing the good fight, but I cannot live without fighting it." The scene ends when Victoria wishes Jamal a safe journey.

Elapsed time: This scene begins at 00:58:32 and ends at 01:00:25 (DVD Scene 19)
Citation: PG-13 for language, sexual/crude humor and battle violence
Citation: *Black Knight* (20th Century Fox, 2001) written by Daryll Quales & Peter Gaulke, directed by Gil Junger

Blazing Saddles   RACISM/DOMINANCE
Bart (Cleavon Little) has been hired as the sheriff of the small town of Rock Ridge; he is charged with defending the town against a gang of bandits (hired by the government) who want to destroy the town and build a railroad on the land. Unfortunately, the townsfolk don't take too kindly to the thought of having a black sheriff.

Lyle (Burton Gilliam) and his team are arriving to a construction site where several Black men and a few Asian men are working on a railroad line. Lyle sarcastically encourages the men to work, "C'mon boys. The way you're lollygagging around here with them picks and shovels, you'd think it was 120 degrees; it can't be more than 114." Just then, one of the Asian men passes out from the heat, and Lyle instructs, "Dock that chink a day's pay for napping on the job." Turning to the many Black men on the work group, Lyle questions why he does not hear any singing: "When you were slaves, you sang like birds. Go on. How about a good old nigger work song?" Bart (Cleavon Little) turns to the other men, and they begin to sing "I Get a Kick Out of You" by Cole Porter, which confuses Lyle and his partners. Lyle begins singing "Swing Low, Sweet Chariot" as an example of such a song, but Bart pretends not to know the song. Lyle then suggests "De Camptown Ladies" and he and his friends begin singing and dancing to the amusement of Bart and his coworkers. Soon, Mr. Taggart (Slim Pickens) interrupts to make everyone get back to work. Taggart has heard of the possibility of quicksand in the direction of the rail line; Lyle offers to take a team of horses to survey the land; he is quickly chided by Taggart who suggests that horses are too valuable. Instead, Taggart argues, "Send over a couple of niggers." Bart and his coworker are sinking in the quicksand when Taggart and Lyle rush up to them. Taggart cries, "Now we are in trouble." Bart looks to his partner, "Oh, *they* in trouble." Taggart instructs Lyle to get a rope. Bart thinks they are going to be rescued, but Lyle lassoes the handcart instead. The scene ends when Bart hits Taggart over the head with a shovel.

Elapsed time: This scene begins at 00:02:30 and ends at 00:08:45 (DVD Scene 2)
Rating: R for some crude language and sexuality.
Citation: *Blazing Saddles* (Crossbow Productions, 1974), screenplay written by Mel Brooks and Norman Steinberg, directed by Mel Brooks

Blazing Saddles   PREJUDICE/DISCRIMINATION
Bart (Cleavon Little) has been hired as the sheriff of the small town of Rock Ridge; he is charged with defending the town against a gang of bandits (hired by the

government) who want to destroy the town and build a railroad on the land. Unfortunately, the townsfolk don't take too kindly to the thought of having a black sheriff.

Bart (Cleavon Little) has been appointed sheriff for the small town of Rock Ridge. The citizens have prepared a parade and celebration in his honor. The town's welcoming committee is practicing their speeches and await confirmation of the sheriff's arrival by a man posted as a lookout. When the lookout gets a clear sight of the new sheriff, who is Black, he tries to say "The sheriff is a nigger" but his voice is drowned out by the playing band; his words are misinterpreted as "the sheriff is near." The lookout even tries to repeat the phrase, but again the music blares. Bart enters the town to the full roars of the crowd, until the people realize he is Black and then they drop dead silent, staring incredulously. The chairman of the welcoming committee begins his speech without looking at Bart, and welcomes him as "our new...nigger." A sign declaring "Welcome Sheriff" is immediately drawn up like a shade on a window. The sheriff pulls the sign back down and begins to read from his official documents from the governor. The citizens draw guns and rifles and threaten Bart. The town's parson asks for peace and someone shoots his Bible. The parson leaves Bart to fend for himself, to wit, Bart draws his own gun on himself and threatens to shoot himself if the people do not leave him alone. Using reverse psychology, Bart backs out of the mob into the safety of the jail. The scene ends when Bart refers to the people as "dumb."

Elapsed time: This scene begins at 00:025:16 and ends at 00:30:20 (DVD Scene 8)
Rating: R for some crude language and sexuality.
Citation: *Blazing Saddles* (Crossbow Productions, 1974), screenplay written by Mel Brooks and Norman Steinberg, directed by Mel Brooks

Borat   **ANTI-SEMITISM**
A fictional documentary following the exploits of Borat (Sacha Baron Cohen) as he travels from his homeland in Kazakhstan to America. He falls in love with superstar Pamela Anderson and travels the country to find her—breaking all the American cultural rules as he travels.

Borat and his cameraman and companion, Azamat, are searching for a place to lodge overnight. After having been rejected by a swanky hotel, they knock on the door of a quaint bed & breakfast. The owners are very hospitable and show the guests around the house. The wife is a painter and is showing Borat many of her paintings of Jews and Jewish life. When she identifies herself as Jewish, Borat grimaces and eerie music begins to play. When they are alone in their room, Borat and Azamat scurry about in fear; they believe that the Jewish couple is going to kill them. The couple brings them food and treats them as honored guests. Later, in the middle of the night, Borat indicates to his video camera that he is "in the nest of Jews" and refers to the Jews' ability to shape shift (referring to the older couple in the shape of human beings). He whispers, "You can barely see their horns. These rats are very clever." Later, he sees two cockroaches on the floor and Azamat states that the Jews have shifted shapes again. They begin throwing money at the roaches and run out of the house screaming down the road. When they get back in the truck, Azamat argues that they should return to New York, "At least there are no Jews there." Borat stops at a gun store to question "What is the best gun to defend from a Jew?" The shop owner hands him a .45 and Borat feels like "Dirty Harold" and says, "Come on and make my day, Jew." The scene ends when the store owner refuses to give him a gun because Borat is not American.

Elapsed time: This scene begins at 00:38:03 and ends at 00:42:15 (DVD Scene 12)
Rating: R for pervasive strong crude and sexual content including graphic nudity, and language
Citation: *Borat* (Dune Entertainment, 2006), written by Sacha Baron Cohen and Anthony Hines, directed by Larry Charles

Boyz N the Hood   **OPPRESSION/OUT GROUP**
Director John Singleton brings us a gritty drama about life in inner city Los Angeles. Sent to live with his father, Tre Styles (Cuba Gooding, Jr) must learn to navigate the mean streets of Compton without succumbing to the violence, crime, and life of poverty surrounding him. He grows up with Ricky (Morris Chestnut), an all star athlete, and his brother Dough Boy (Ice Cube); together they try to make sense of the world around them.

Furious Styles (Laurence Fishburne) is giving his son Tre and his friends a lesson on the racial patterns of neighborhood gentrification. He schools the young men on how their criminal activities are driving the property values down. "If they bring the property value down, they can buy the land at a lower price. Then they move the people out, raise the property value, and sell at a profit." He continues, "What we need to do is keep everything in our neighborhood; everything black. Black owned with black money—just like the Jews, the Italians, the Mexicans and Koreans do." An older gentleman interrupts that it is no one from outside the community bringing the values down, but these young teens with their drug behaviors and violence. Furious questions how the drugs enter the black community, "We don't own any planes. We don't own no ships. We are not the people who are flying and floating that shit in here. I know every time you turn on the TV that's what you see—black people selling the rock. But that wasn't a problem as long as it was here; it wasn't a problem until it was in Iowa and it showed up on Wall Street where there are hardly any black people." Furious regards the trafficking of guns as an external conspiracy as well. He questions the preponderance of liquor stores in the black neighborhood; "Why? Because they want us to kill ourselves. You go out to Beverly Hills, you don't see that shit." He continues, "The best way to destroy a people is you take away their ability to reproduce themselves. Who is it that is dying on these streets every night? Y'all. Young brothers like yourselves." He tells a young man, "You have to think, young brother, about your future."

Elapsed time: This scene begins at 01:03:56 and ends at 01:06:25 (DVD Scene 18)
Rating: R for language, violence, and sexuality
Citation: *Boyz N the Hood* (Columbia Pictures, 1991), written and directed by John Singleton

Braveheart   PRIVILEGE/POWER

Scotsman William Wallace (Mel Gibson) pledges himself to fight against English tyranny after his wife is murdered by an Englishman. Although he is captured and disemboweled, Wallace's cries of "Freedom" encourage his compatriots to continue fighting and win the war.

William (Mel Gibson) and the townsfolk are celebrating the marriage of two if its own. Soon, a squad of soldiers rides in on their horses and the commander announces that he has come "to claim the right of *prima noctes*. As lord of these lands, I will bless this marriage by taking the bride into my bed on the 'first night' of her union." The bride's father and her husband both protest, but are subdued by the soldiers. The leader proclaims, "It is my noble right." The scene ends as the bride rides away with the soldiers.

Elapsed time: This scene begins at 00:26:10 and ends at 00:28:30 (DVD Scene 4)
Rating: R for brutal medieval warfare
Citation: *Braveheart* (Paramount Pictures, 1995), written by Randall Wallace, directed by Mel Gibson

Bringing Down the House   IN-GROUP

Legendary comedian Steve Martin plays Phil Sanderson, a trust attorney who is trying to land the ultra-conservative and super rich client, Mrs. Arness. All is in order until Phil agrees to help Charlene (Queen Latifah), an escaped convict clear her name.

Phil has invited Mrs. Arness (Joan Plowright) to his home for dinner and to sign the contracts (Mrs. Arness actually wants to check him out; she has heard rumors that Sanderson's personal life is out of whack, and she refuses to place her money with an unstable attorney). At dinner, Mrs. Arness meets Charlene (Queen Latifah), who is an escaped convict posing as Sanderson's nanny and housekeeper. Charlene's cooking reminds Arness about her childhood and she begins to relate stories about her former maid, Ivy. She describes how Ivy worked for no money, only the scraps of food left over after the family ate. Arness begins singing a "Negro spiritual" that Ivy's brother sang, "Mama, is Massa gonna sell me tomorrow? Yes! Yes!" Both Charlene and the Sanderson family are disturbed by the stories. The scene ends when Sanderson returns from the bathroom.

Elapsed time: This scene begins at 01:06:30 and ends at 01:15:15 (DVD Scene 8)
Rating: PG-13 for language, sexual humor and drug material
Citation: *Bringing Down the House* (Touchstone Pictures, 2002), written by Jason Filardi, directed by Adam Shankman

A Bug's Life   OPPRESSION

Intent on saving his ant colony from a swarm of overbearing grasshoppers, Flik (voiced by comedian Dave Foley) enlists the help of a team of insects who are lost circus troupe performances. They are successful in routing their enemies and restoring the ant colony.

The ant colony is in an uproar as they anxiously await the arrival of the dreaded grasshoppers who demand an annual offering of food. To the ants, the grasshoppers have only one purpose- "They come, they eat, they leave." Flik, a bumbling ant, accidentally lost of the grasshoppers' food, and the grasshoppers are none too thrilled. The grasshoppers burst into the colony and the ants scramble in fear. Hopper, the head of the grasshoppers, storms about the colony taking a menacing stance. He speaks angrily for having to "come down to your level" to look for his food. He tells the princess that it is a "bu122212g-eat-bug world out there" with a pecking order—"The sun grows the food. The ants pick the food. The grasshoppers eat the food." Hopper violently stifles his own brother for indicating how the birds eat the grasshoppers (and tells the story of how Hopper was almost eaten by a bird once). In his anger, Hopper punches another grasshopper instead of his brother. In his "compassion" Hopper gives the ants another chance to fulfill his food order in spite of the queen ant's request to have time to hunt for food for the any colony. He threatens to remove his "protection" of the colony which would leave the ants prey for other insects—"Someone could get hurt," Hopper snaps and then reveals a maniacal grasshopper on a leash whom Hopper taunts with a small ant. Flik attempts to rescue the ant, but Hopper demands he get back in line. Hopper states, "It seems to me that you ants are forgetting your place" and then doubles the order of food. The scene ends when Hopper and the other grasshoppers leave the ant colony.

Elapsed time: This scene begins at 00:09:52 and ends at 00:15:10 (DVD Scene 4)
Rating: G for general audiences
Citation: *A Bug's Life* (Pixar Animation Studios, 1998) written by John Lasseter & Andrew Stanton, directed by John Lasseter

A Bug's Life   OPPRESSION, IN GROUP

Intent on saving his ant colony from a swarm of overbearing grasshoppers, Flik (voiced by comedian Dave Foley) enlists the help of a team of insects who are lost circus troupe performances. They are successful in routing their enemies and restoring the ant colony.

Hopper, the leader of the grasshoppers is being questioned by the other grasshoppers regarding what they feel is unnecessary treatment of the ant colony. Hopper responds that although they have enough grain for the winter, the grasshoppers must return to the ant colony because "there was that one ant that stood up to me." The other grasshoppers respond that it was only one ant who stepped up. To demonstrate why he is so concerned, Hopper throws a piece of grain at one of the grasshoppers and asked him if the grain hurt; the grasshopper dismisses the tiny piece of grain. Hopper then pulls the cap off the grain dispenser and overwhelms the grasshopper: "You let one ant stand up to us and they all might stand up. Those puny little ants outnumber us 100 to 1. And if they ever figure out, there goes our way of life. It's not about food. It's about keeping those ants in line."

Elapsed time: This scene begins at 00:53:23 and ends at 00:56:25 (DVD Scene 20)
Rating: G for general audiences
Citation: *A Bug's Life* (Pixar Animation Studios, 1998) written by John Lasseter & Andrew Stanton, directed by John Lasseter

Charlie Wilson's War   PRIVILEGE

Congressman Charlie Wilson (Tom Hanks) is one politician who knows how to grease the wheels. Most of his votes go to the highest paying lobbyist, that is, until he is persuaded by a wealthy contributor, Joanne Herring (Julia Roberts) to pay attention to the war in the Middle East. Through his covert dealings, Wilson was able to bring much needed aid to the Afghan soldiers and bring an effective end to their war with the Soviet Union.

Congressman Wilson's assistant, Bonnie, is briefing the senator about a disgruntled constituent who is in his office to discuss the presence of a nativity scene on public property when they are stopped by a staff member of another senator. The page asks Wilson if he would be willing to serve on an ethics committee to help a scandal-ridden senator escape prosecution. Wilson chuckles, "Well, Jesus, Donnelly, everyone in town knows I'm on the other side of that issue." In fact, Wilson says, "If anyone asks what the hell I'm doing on the ethics committee, we'll just tell them I like chasing women and drinking whiskey and the Speaker felt we were underrepresented." Speaking of his boss's gratitude, Donnelly adds, "Tip's gonna want to return the favor. So, if anything comes up that you'd like me to speak with him about, please..." Wilson jumps in with a request to be appointed to the board of directors of the Kennedy Center because "It's a great place to take a date, and I can never afford the tickets." Donnelly responds, "Consider it done" and walks away. The congressman then turns to the newswires to find out what's going on in the world. Bonnie asks "Why can't you wait for newspapers like everybody else?" Wilson contends, "Cause I think it's productive to know today's news today; and it makes me one day smarter than you, which I enjoy as well." The scene ends as Charlie enters the voting room.

Elapsed time: This scene begins at 00:08:06 and ends at 00:10:14 (DVD Scene 3)
Rating: R for strong language, nudity, sexual content, and some drug use
Citation: *Charlie Wilson's War* (Universal Pictures, 2007), screenplay written by Aaron Sorkin, directed by Mike Nichols

The Chosen   ANTI-SEMITISM

Set in the 1940s and based on the best-selling novel by the Chaim Potok, The Chosen follows two Jewish friends, one a son of an ultra-orthodox rabbi, the other is a son of a more secular father. Danny, a member of the orthodox Hasidim must decide whether allegiance to his father's way of life is most important, or whether his friendship with Reuven is paramount.

Danny (Barry Miller) and Reuven (Robbie Benson) are walking down the street discussing whether it is appropriate for a Jewish person to study and learn the German language given the role of the Nazis in the Holocaust when they are accosted by several young men who threaten violence and refer to them as "kikes." One of the boys makes fun of the traditional curly hair of Hasidic Jews and refers to Danny as "Honey." Danny ends up punching one of the young men before he and Reuven run away.

Elapsed time: This scene begins at 00:37:05 and ends at 00:38:08 (DVD Scene 8)
Rating: PG for thematic material
Citation: *The Chosen* (20th Century Fox, 1981), screenplay written by Edwin Gordon, directed by Jeremy Kagan

Coach Carter OUT-GROUP
Hell-bent on ensuring his student athletes have a chance for survival that does not include selling drugs or gang violence, one high school basketball coach has the chutzpah to dare the students to thrive academically. His controversial policies of academics before athletics angers many parents and members of the local community, but his students find the ability to achieve in both arenas.

Ken Carter (Samuel L. Jackson) has just accepted the position of head basketball coach at his alma mater, Richmond High School, and is being introduced to his new squad by the former coach. In his interactions with the student athletes, Coach Carter is no-nonsense; he gives respect and commands it from his students. He refers to each of the gentlemen as "Sir," and expects the same of them. One of the players, Jason Lyle (Channing Tatum), rejects being called this moniker—"I ain't no sir," he said. Unlike his predecessor, Coach Carter sets high academic standards and requires the students to sign contracts to agree to go to all classes and achieve high academic marks. Most of the students grouse at these expectations and begin to make disparaging comments about the coach. One of the students quips, "Yo, this is a country-ass nigga, dog," referring to Coach Carter. When the coach questions the statement, another student, Timo Cruz, adds, "Worm was just wondering—are you some country church nigga with your tie on and all that?" Coach Carter indicates the importance of showing one another respect, and the inappropriateness of using the term "nigga" (a euphemism for nigger). Timo (Rick Gonzalez) tells Carter that even "God ain't gonna do you no good in this neighborhood." Timo makes fun of Carter's propriety—"Sir, can you believe this uppity Negro, sir?" Coach Carter bristles at Timo's disrespect and ejects him from the squad. The scene ends when Cruz and two other players leave the court.

Elapsed time: This scene begins at 00:08:44 and ends at 00:14:00 (DVD Scene 3)
Rating: PG-13 for violence, sexual content, language, teen partying, and some drug material

Citation: *Coach Carter* (Paramount Pictures, 20055), written by Mark Schwan & John Gatins, directed by Thomas Carter

The Color Purple OUT-GROUP/SEXISM

Celie (Whoopi Goldberg) is in a loveless and abusive marriage to Mister (Danny Glover) who is in love with another woman. Celie searches for love, respect, and fulfillment despite the numerous odds stacked against her. Based on the critically acclaimed novel of the same title by Alice Walker.

Harpo (Willard Pugh) is seeking advice from his father (Glover) about how to best assert his position as husband to his wife Sophia. Mister asks Harpo, "Do you ever hit her?" When Harpo suggests that he does not, Mister questions, "How do you expect her to mind?" He continues, "Wives is like children. You have to let them know who got the upper hand. Nothing can do it better than a good, sound beating. Sophia thinks too much of herself. She needs to be taken down a peg or two." Later, while Sophia (Oprah Winfrey) and Celie (Goldberg) are gardening, Harpo comes running up and demands that Sophia make him something to eat; Sophia dismisses him by handing him the hoe and commanding, "Make yourself useful" and walks away. Befuddled, Harpo asks Celie, "What am I going to do about Sophia?" Celie answers "Beat her." Soon Sophia comes storming through the cornstalks to where Celie is standing and argues, "You told Harpo to beat me! All my life I had to fight. I had to fight my daddy; I had to fight my uncles. I had to fight my brothers. Girl child ain't safe in a family of mens. But I ain't never thought I had to fight in my own house. I loves Harpo; God knows I do, but I'll kill him dead before I let him beta me. You want a dead son-in-law Miss Celie? You keep in advising him like you doing." Celie fearfully returns, "This life be over soon; heaven last always." Sophia answers, "You oughta bash Mister's head open and think about heaven later." The scene ends when Sophia marches off.

Elapsed time: This scene begins at 00:41:58 and ends at 00:44:50 (DVD Scene 12)
Rating: PG-13 for some violence, language, and sexual content
Citation: *The Color Purple* (Warner Bros. Pictures, 1985) screenplay written by Menno Meyjes, directed by Steven Spielberg

The Condemned CO-OPTATION

Reality television takes a gruesome turn when one executive brings condemned killers to a remote island in a kill-or-be-killed "game" where the last man or woman alive wins freedom and a pot of money. One of the contestants, Jack Conrad ("Stone Cold" Steve Austin), is a decorated military hero who will stop at nothing to survive and take down the greedy executive.

Breck (Robert Mammone) is being interviewed by a national television news anchorwoman regarding his controversial reality television show when he is interrupted by two of his assistants. They tell Breck that one of his headliners has been "lost." As he enters the compound headquarters, Breck complains "They shot my Arab? We had him on the mainland and they shot my fucking Arab?"

The assistant tries to reassure Breck, "Relax, OK. We got a replacement." The replacement is a "Hardcore Guatemalan—convicted of 13 torture killings. He's ready to go." Breck yells, "I don't want a fucking Guatemalan; I already got two Mexicans." Moving over to a large map, he explains, "This is the Arab world. If they don't have anybody to cheer for, they don't log on. I want a fucking Arab! A child-killing, Koran-ranting, suicide bombing Arab!" The assistant informs Breck of a possible candidate, "A 6'7" Islamic fundamentalist. He's ours if we want him." The scene ends as the crew is sent to the prison to retrieve the new prisoner.

Elapsed time: This scene begins at 00:08:42 and ends at 00:10:10 (DVD Scene 3)
Rating: R for pervasive strong brutal violence, and for language
Citation: *The Condemned* (Lionsgate Films, 2007), written by Scott Wiper & Rob Hedden, directed by Scott Wiper

Coneheads   **DIFFERENCE/ETHNOCENTRISM**
Dan Akroyd and Jane Curtin bring their hilarious Saturday Night Live sketch to the big screen Akroyd stars as Beldar Conehead, and alien from outer space, who tries to introduce his family of cylindrical craniums to the citizens of Earth.

Gorman Seedling (Michael McKean) and his assistant Eli Turnbull (David Spade) are Immigration and Naturalization Service agents who are trying to prove that Beldar and his family are not only illegal aliens, but also from outer space. In this scene, Seedling and Turnbull pose as ministers from the local Kingdom Hall of Jehovah's Witnesses and are invited into Beldar's home under the guise of sharing their faith. Beldar and Prymaat (Curtin) are preparing to attend a masquerade ball and are dressed in costumes. Seedling asks, "Do you agree that the world's headed towards a terrible calamity?" Beldar confirms "direct personal knowledge" of such a coup. Beldar wonders, "What do you know of the doom awaiting this planet?" Seedling adds, "As Jehovah's Witnesses, we believe the end of the world is approaching and that only 144,000 people will be saved." Prymaat argues that she does not believe it will be that many. Beldar argues that 144,000 "is a very optimistic estimate considering the primitive weapons the earth people will use for their defense." Seedling adds, "When the time comes, no weapon of this earth will avail mankind;" both Beldar and Prymaat agree. Seedling questions where Beldar and Prymaat are from; Prymaat answers, "We come from France" and Beldar chimes in, "but we're American citizens now." Seedling asks for proof when Connie, the Coneheads' daughter enters. Seedling asks if she was born in the United States, and Beldar begins to answer, "Yes, she is native to your pla...uh, country." Assuming they are lying, Seedling asks questions in the French language; Beldar and Prymaat respond appropriately. The scene ends when Beldar ejects the two visitors from his home after receiving an important phone call.

Elapsed time: This scene begins at 00:56:26 and ends at 00:59:17 (DVD Scene 10)
Rating: PG for comic nudity and some double entendre humor
Citation: *Coneheads* (Paramount Pictures, 1993) written by Tom Davis & Dan Akroyd, directed by Steve Barron

The Contender   SOCIAL JUSTICE

Senator Laine Hanson (Joan Allen) has been nominated to be the vice president designate of the United States of America, but faces strong opposition from her colleagues on Capitol Hill who resent the president's choice of the female candidate. Her brutal confirmation hearings reveal bias and bigotry at all levels of the government.

The President of the United States (Jeff Bridges) appears before the Congress to scold them for mishandling the confirmation hearings of Senator Hanson. He equates their opposition to treason and calls for an immediate confirmation of Senator Hanson, although she has requested to withdraw her nomination. He explains, "Your leadership has raised the stakes of hate to a level where can no longer separate the demagogue from the truly inspired." His harshest remarks were reserved for those "traitors to the necessary end result: that of righteousness, the truth—the concept of making the American dream blind to gender." He continues speaking, "You come at us with whatever weapons that you have in your arsenal but there is no weapon as powerful as that of an idea whose time has come: a woman will serve in the highest level of the Executive. Simple as that." After announcing that he will not accept Hanson's resignation, the president praises Hanson, "Greatness. It comes in many forms. Sometimes it comes in the form of sacrifice. That's the loneliest form. Now it turns out that Laine Hanson is a woman; an American of devout principle, and she has inspired me to act alike." The president calls for a live confirmation vote so that he can visibly "see who would eliminate the possibility of greatness in American leadership because of lies, half truths and innuendoes. I will not be deterred by partisanship. I will not be deterred by misogyny. I will not be deterred by hate. You have now come face-to-face with my will. Confirm my nominee. Heal this nation and let the American people explode into the new millennium with the exhilaration of being true to the glory of this democracy.

Elapsed time: This scene begins at 01:54:00 and ends at 01:59:00 (DVD Scene 19)
Rating: R for strong sexual content and language
Citation: *The Contender* (DreamWorks Pictures, 2000), written and directed by Rod Lurie

Cursed   IN-GROUP/OPPRESSION/HOMOPHOBIA
Horror master Wes Craven satisfies the bloodlust in all of us as Ellie (Christina Ricci) and her brother, Jimmy, learn that they have been infected and are changing into werewolves. The Los Angeles night life just got a little more interesting!

Bo, a textbook "jock," constantly teases Jimmy, who is a bit nerdy. In a previous scene, Jimmy is bitten by a werewolf and his strength has been increasing. In this scene, Jimmy is having a conversation with one of the cheerleaders while the wrestling team is practicing. Soon Bo approaches and asks the young lady [referring to Jimmy], "Are you going fruit fly on me?" Jimmy shoos him away, but Bo tells him, "Oh, you are asking for it Abercrombie." Jimmy snaps back,

"Bo, you're really becoming transparent. How about a little identity intervention, ok? All of this internalized homophobia is just giving you away." Bo pushes Jimmy and tells him, "You better watch your ass." Soon, the wrestling coach intervenes, but Bo tells him that Jimmy wants to try out for the wrestling team. Jimmy's opponent, Louie, states, "Ok, limp wrist, stay away from my groin." Voices from the crowd call Jimmy a "girly man," and question "who let that sissy on the floor," and warn "never get on top of a fairy, man" when Jimmy is pinned. Someone else yells, "Watch his nails, Lou; he might scratch your eyes out." Soon, Bo and Jimmy are preparing to wrestle and Bo states, "C'mon fairy, shake your dust." Jimmy returns, "You'd like that wouldn't you?" Bo gets him in a hold from behind and asks, "C'mon fag, what do you like that?" Moments later, Jimmy lifts Bo above his head and tells him, "You know the best part about being a fairy? You get to fly." He slams Bo to the ground and the crowd cheers to end the scene.

Elapsed time: This scene begins at 00:44:24 and ends at 00:47:40 (DVD Scene 7)
Rating: R for language
Citation: *Cursed (*Dimension Films, 2005), written by Kevin Williamson, and directed by Wes Craven

Daddy Day Camp   DIFFERENCE
Charlie (Cuba Gooding, Jr.) and Phil (Paul Rae) have recently purchased the grounds of their childhood summer camp. Unfortunately, neither of them are very good at camping and have even less experience with children; not to mention the numerous repairs that need to be made before the camp will pass all the legal red tape. Can they get their act together in time for the campers to compete against the neighboring camp for rich kids?

On opening day of their new day camp, Charlie and Phil have a full house of kids. They are trying (unsuccessfully) to corral them into groups. The students are complaining about their assigned groupings. One student argues, "I'm older than these babies. I should be in that group." A lone boy in a group of all girls states, "I didn't sign up to be with no skirts. They got cooties." A girl in that groups suggests, "There's no such thing as cooties. It's simply a term used to express age-appropriate discomfort of those not of our gender." The scene ends with a complete melee of children and staff members.

Elapsed time: This scene begins at 00:15:35 and ends at 00:17:49 (DVD Scene 6)
Rating: PG for mild bodily humor and language
Citation: *Daddy Day Camp* (Tristar Pictures & Revolution Studios, 2007), screenplay by Geoff Rodkey, J. David Stein, & David Weiss, directed by Fred Savage

Dangerous Minds   DOMINANCE
An ex-marine teacher struggles to connect with her students in an inner city school. She battles apathy, crime, and a system that expected failure. Based on the true story My Posse Don't Do Homework by Louann Johnson.

Louann Johnson (Michelle Pfeiffer) is sitting in the assistant principal's office bemoaning the fact that her star pupil Callie has gotten pregnant, and Ms. Johnson believes that the school board is requiring Callie to attend a mother-to-be program at a different school. The principal reveals that this school move is not a policy, but a "preference" of the principals who believe that removing these pregnant students is better because "it [pregnancy] is not a warning, Louann, it's prestige, it's stardom…not all of these girls become pregnant by accident. Pregnancy is contagious." Ms. Johnson disgustedly replies, "So you make them think that they have to leave. You just push them out a little earlier; make it a little harder, make it a little more hopeless."

Elapsed time: This scene begins at 01:08:49 and ends at 01:10:30 (DVD Scene 10)
Rating: R for language
Citation: *Dangerous Minds* (Simpson & Bruckheimer Films, 1995), screenplay by Ronald Bass, and directed by John N. Smith

Dazed and Confused   **DOMINANCE**
The incoming class of freshmen at a Texas high school comes face to face with the outgoing senior class on the last day of school in 1976. The seniors dish out some serious hazing, especially the senior girls. The seniors are amused as they look to leave their mark on high school life.

In the parking lot of the local high school, members of the female senior class have gathered several dozen of the freshmen females for some ritual hazing. Darla, the ring leader, enters the center of the ring and announces, "All right you little freshmen bitches! Air raid!" The air raid required the girls to lay prostrate on the cement. When the students did not move fast enough, they were berated into repeatedly doing the action. The girls were called "pathetic," "horrible slut girls," "freshmen sluts," and other demoralizing words. Tony and Mike, two men watching the melee question the appropriateness of the activity, Mike ponders, "What's fascinating is the way not only the school, but the entire community seems to be supporting this or turn their heads. I mean, they apparently have permission to use the school parking lot, no parents seem to mind; they're selling concessions." Darla speaking to her plebes says, "We gave you all a chance, but since you little prick teases can't follow instructions, we're just going to have to try something else, won't we? You love us. Smile. You love us." The senior women begin to dump all types of foodstuffs (eggs, ketchup, mustard, flour, oatmeal, etc) all over the young women who are still on the ground. The freshmen are required to open their mouths while the seniors pour goop in their mouths. [War's "Why Can't We Be Friends" plays in the background]. Some of the young women have dog leashes placed around their necks and are made to kneel before the on-looking men and propose marriage. Some of the boys make lewd, suggestive comments about oral sex while the girls are on their knees. While laughing, one of the boys suggests that the comments were degrading and horrible. One of the seniors quietly mentions to the freshmen, "I just want you guys to know I feel for you, man; I did it when I was a freshman, and you'll do it when you're a senior. Now fry like bacon, you little freshmen piggies!" A young girl is required to bow before Tony and Mike and propose. After "imagining the possibilities" of the girl's promise to do whatever he wishes, Mike tells the young lady "we were just discussing the utter stupidity of these initiation rituals, and we were wondering why someone like you would subject yourself to the losing end of it all." Before she could answer, the senior woman interrupts: "What are we having a social hour over here? I'm supposed to be being a bitch. Back to the pit!" Darla beckons, "OK girlies, it's hot out here and I am sick of looking at all of you, so let's just get out of here." The scene ends as they force the girls onto a truck.

Elapsed time: This scene begins at 00:20:05 and ends at 00:24:10 (DVD Scene 3)
Rating: R for pervasive, continuous teen drug and alcohol use and very strong language
Citation: *Dazed & Confused* (Alphaville Films, 1993) written and directed by Richard Linklater

Dirty Dancing   POWER/CLASSISM/OUT-GROUP
Johnny Castle is the dance instructor at an exclusive summer camp for rich socialites. Growing up on the wrong side of the tracks from his clients, Johnny has a reputation for being a bad boy among some of the women. When he begins dating one of the summer guests, Johnny's way of life is threatened, but he remains determined to win the heart of his love and that of her snobbish father.

Baby (Jennifer Grey) and Johnny (Patrick Swayze) are alone in the dance studio; Baby, a guest at the resort, and Johnny, the dance instructor, have been having a secret and forbidden love affair and in this scene Johnny is trying to have his way with Baby who resists his advances. They are interrupted by Neil Kellerman (Lonnie Price), the grandson of the owner. Neil informs Johnny that he has been appointed to direct the final performance of the summer and has plans to "shake things up and move with the times" a little by changing the final dance number. Johnny is excited to offer ideas on how to add Latin rhythms to the show; Neil interrupts stating, "Whoa boy; this is way over your head." Neil recommends closing the summer with the Pechanga instead of the mambo, and when Johnny doesn't gibe with this idea, Neil threatens, "Well, you're free to do the same tired number as last year, if you want, but next year we'll find another dance person who'll only be too happy..." Johnny acquiesces. Later Baby asks Johnny, "Why did you let him talk to you that way?" Johnny quips, "What do you mean, fight the boss man?" Baby suggests that Neil is a "person just like everyone else," but Johnny maintains, "Look, I know these people. They are rich and they're mean. They won't listen to me." Baby asks, "Why not fight harder? Make them listen." Johnny answers, "Because I need this goddamned job lined up for next summer" as he does not want to work as a house painter with his father and uncle. They continue walking but Baby suddenly pulls Johnny to the ground because she does not want her father and sister to see her with him. This angers Johnny: "Fight harder, huh? I don't see you fighting so hard telling your daddy that I'm your guy." Baby counters, "I will, but with my father, it's complicated." Johnny tells her, "I don't think that you ever had any intention of telling him—ever." The scene ends when Johnny storms away.

Elapsed time: This scene begins at 01:06:33 and ends at 01:11:00 (DVD Scene 20)
Rating: PG-13 for language and sensuality
Citation: *Dirty Dancing* (Artisan Entertainment, 1987) written by Eleanor Bergstein, directed by Emile Ardolino

Dr. Seuss' Horton Hears a Who   DOMINANCE/INVISIBILITY

Dr. Seuss' classic tale of an elephant who can hear the tiny citizens of Who-ville who love on a floating speck of dust comes to life. Horton begins a campaign to protect the tiny community from any harm. Featuring the voices of Jim Carrey, Steve Carrell, Seth Rogen, Carol Burnett, and Amy Poehler.

Kangaroo (Burnett) has a major problem with Horton's protection of the tiny citizens of Who-ville; in fact, she does not believe there is such a community. She breaks through the bushes and declares to the others, "What is happening in the jungle of Nool? There once was a time when people were people and specks were specks. Well, I say, if can't see it, hear it, or feel it, it doesn't exist." She continues, as if making an appeal, "Our way of life is under attack. And who's leading the attack? Horton!" Mouse comes to Horton's defense and proclaims that Horton would not hurt a fly, "except for that fly city he sat on; but he didn't do that on purpose." Kangaroo hushes him and continues on her tirade, "Are we going to let troublemakers like Horton poison the minds of our children?" The suggestion that the children will be affected by Horton's beliefs causes a stir, and Kangaroo adds, "When Horton tells the children about worlds beyond the jungle, he makes them question authority, which leads to defiance, which leads to anarchy!" An ape yells, "Yeah! Horton must pay!" Another animal argues, "It's that speck! We have to do something!" Another agrees, "For the children!" Kangaroo yells, "Are we going to let him get away with this?" All the animals yell, "No" and begin scrambling around in search of Horton.

Elapsed time: This scene begins at 01:05:30 and ends at 01:06:55 (DVD Scene 26)
Rating: G for general audiences
Citation: *Dr. Seuss' Horton Hears a Who* (20th Century Fox Animation, 2008), screenplay written by Cinco Paul & Ken Daurio, directed by Jimmy Hayward & Steve Martino

Dumb & Dumber   CO-OPTATION

Lloyd and Harry are two dim-witted friends on a cross country trek to return a briefcase full of cash to its rightful owner who is on her way to Aspen, Colorado. The two unwittingly become embroiled in a kidnapping and ransom case that leaves the two of them in serious danger.

Lloyd Christmas (Jim Carrey) and his roommate and best friend, Harry Dunne (Jeff Daniels) are down on their luck and are in need of cash. They are frustrated by the lack of jobs in their local town, "unless you want to work 40 hours a week." Lloyd prepares to go to the grocery store and Harry tells him to only purchase the essentials because that is the last of their money. Later, Lloyd is walking down the street with two cases of beer, a large 10 gallon foam cowboy hat, pinwheels, and other items. He stops to purchase a pornographic magazine but accidentally leaves his wallet inside the magazine holder. He does not have additional change to open the box; an elderly woman in a motorized wheelchair stops by and Lloyd asks if she can change a dollar. Unable to, she agrees to watch over his purchases while he goes to get change. Lloyd thanks her and adds, "Hey, I guess they're right. Senior citizens, although slow and dangerous behind the wheel, can still serve a purpose." He walks away from her and says, "Don't you go dying on me." Later, Lloyd tells Harry that the old woman stole all of his groceries.

Elapsed time: This scene begins at 00:13:58 and ends at 00:16:05 (DVD Scene 4)
Rating: PG-13 for off color humor
Citation: *Dumb & Dumber* (New Line Cinema, 1994, Peter & Bobby Farrelly and Bennett Yellin, directed by Peter Farrelly

Equilibrium   OPPRESSION/POWER
In the future, society has found a way to eliminate war by outlawing human emotion. Books, art, literature, and other forms of entertainment become contraband and all citizens must take a medicine that will suppress all feelings. Christian Bale plays John Preston, a soldier who is charged with ensuring compliance with the rules of the new world; that is, until he skips a dose of the medicine that controls him.

Speaking to his subjects in the world called Libria, Dupont (Angus Macfayden) congratulates the Librians for achieving peace in their world. He states, "At last, war is a word whose meaning fades from our understanding. At last, we are whole." Dupont speaks of the "disease in the heart of man" which results in anger, hate, war, and rage. Scenes of the Rodney King beating, Hitler and the Nazi regime, and images of war play above the heads of the citizens as Dupont speaks to them. Dupont indicates that the cause of the disease is "human emotion." He speaks of the Librian "embracing" the cure to the "abysmal lows" of human emotions—a drug called Prozium. At once, all the citizens take an injection of the drug as they are surrounded by soldiers with assault weapons. Dupont narrates "Now we are at peace with ourselves, and humankind is one. War is gone. Hate a memory. We are our own conscience now." As Dupont is speaking, a young boy points at an older citizen and two armed soldiers forcefully take the old man away. "And it is this conscience," Dupont continues, "that guides us to rate EC-10 for emotional content all those things that might tempt us to feel again and destroy them." Piles of video tapes and reels bearing the label EC-10 are torched. To the sounds of tumultuous cheers, Dupont shouts, "Librians, you have won. Against all odds and your own natures, you have survived."

Elapsed time: This scene begins at 00:08:22 and ends at 00:10:40 (DVD Scene 2)
Rating: R for violence
Citation: *Equilibrium* (Dimension Films, 2002) written and directed by Kurt Wimmer

The Family Stone   DIFFERENCE/OUT-GROUP/IN-GROUP
The Stone family unites for a common cause when their favorite son brings his uptight girlfriend home for the Christmas holiday, with plans of proposing. Overwhelmed by the hostile reception, she begs her sister to join her for emotional support, triggering further complications.

Everett is the favored son of the Stone family and he has brought his girlfriend, Meredith, home to meet his family. Meredith (Sarah Jessica Parker) and Everett (Dermot Mulroney) are arguing about how ill-received she has been by Everett's family. In the previous scene, one of Everett's sisters scolded Meredith for her actions during a game of charades. Here, Meredith shows how poorly she is treated in comparison to Everett, "The natives would never dream of letting their god sleep on a couch. Not when they have me to blame." She explains her concern that Everett may also be mistreating her: "I can see you beginning to look at me like they do." Everett denies it, but she continues by saying "It isn't? You're telling me you're not wondering why you brought me here...that you're not beginning to have doubts? That you don't wish I were different?" Mr. & Mrs. Stone (Craig T. Nelson, Diane Keaton) are in their bedroom talking about Everett and Meredith. Mr. Stone questions, "Well, what I don't understand is what he sees in her." He explains that she is a good catch for her manners, language, and social class, but is interrupted by Mrs. Stone who says, "You stick a silver spoon up any monkey's butt, it's bound to go 'please' and 'thank you.' Big deal." Mr. Stone continues his "defense" by stating that Meredith does not know herself very well, "which means, I'm afraid, that our Everett may not know himself at all."

Elapsed time: This scene begins at 00:20:48 and ends at 00:22:51 (DVD Scene 10)
Rating: PG-13 for some sexual content including dialogue, and drug references
Citation: *The Family Stone* (Fox 2000 Pictures, 2005), written and directed by Thomas Bezucha

Finding Forrester   DOMINANCE
Jamal Wallace, an African American teenage male, who lives in the inner city, is offered a basketball scholarship to an elite private prep school. He is athletically talented, but he is also a gifted writer. He meets William Forrester, a reclusive author, who befriends him and coaches him to become a better writer.

Prof. Crawford (F. Murray Abraham) is talking to a student named John Coleridge (Michael Pitt) in the classroom. He is belittling John for his inability to answer a question. Crawford argues that John should know the name of the author in question; the student is stumped but Jamal (Rob Brown) jumps in and answers correctly. Crawford says, "Perhaps your skills do extend farther than the basketball court." Jamal takes the liberty to correct Professor Crawford's misuse of grammar. Naturally, Crawford takes offense and begins to grill Jamal with additional questions—Jamal aces them all, much to Professor Crawford's dismay. Crawford ultimately dismisses Jamal from the classroom for impudence. The scene ends when Claire (Anna Paquin) tells Jamal, "You have no idea what Crawford does to students who do this."

Elapsed time: This scene begins at 01:34:11 and ends at 01:38:58 (DVD Scene 23)
Rating: PG-13 for brief strong language and some sexual references
Citation: *Finding Forrester* (Columbia Pictures, 2000), written by Mike Rich, directed by Gus Van Sant

Finding Forrester   CO-OPTATION

Jamal Wallace (Rob Brown), an African American teenage male, who lives in the inner city, is offered a basketball scholarship to an elite private prep school. He is athletically talented, but he is also a gifted writer. He meets William Forrester, a reclusive author, who befriends him and coaches him to become a better writer.

Jamal and his mother have been invited to a meeting with Dr. Simon, the principal of his public high school. Because of Jamal's high academic achievement, he has been accepted to an elite private preparatory school, the Mailor-Callow School in Manhattan, "where only the best go." Mr. Bradley, Mailor's administrator, tells Jamal's mother that the family will not have to worry about paying for the expensive school. Bradley adds, "Jamal, when Dr. Simon said 'Only the best go to Mailor,' he neglected to mention that our commitment to excellence extends beyond the classroom." Jamal answers, "I figured that." Bradley returns, "We thought you might." Turning to Mrs. Wallace, Bradley informs, "about 40 of our students have gone on to play college ball; three have made it to the professional level. We took the liberty of evaluating your play last year. While this is strictly an academic offer, we won't be disappointed if you choose to play. All we ask is you come out for a few days, take a look, think it over." The scene ends when Mr. Bradley gets into his car.

Elapsed time: This scene begins at 00:24:11 and ends at 00:26:20 (DVD Scene 7)
Rating: PG-13 for brief strong language and some sexual references
Citation: *Finding Forrester* (Columbia Pictures, 2000), written by Mike Rich, directed by Gus Van Sant

Fools Rush In   ETHNOCENTRISM

After a very brief courtship with Alex Whitman (Matthew Perry), Isabela Fuentes (Salma Hayek) learns that she is pregnant and the impetuous couple get married in Las Vegas. Their new love is tested by cross cultural differences, language, socioeconomic class—can their marriage survive?

Isabela (Salma Hayek) is having a discussion with her friend, Lanie (Siobhan Fallon), are preparing dinner and discussing Isabel's family's reaction to the announcement that she had gotten married when Alex (Matthew Perry) and his business partner, Jeff (Jon Tenney) enter the kitchen. Lanie makes a comment about Alex's institutional style of décor at his apartment. Alex mentions that he only plans to live there for the next few months; when his construction project is done, he is planning to move from Nevada to New York. Isabel mentions "I like it here. My family is here; my friends are here. And my work is here. You can't raise a baby in that city." Alex counters, "People do it all the time. Have you ever been there?" Isabel returns, "And you've never been off the strip. There's more to Nevada than Vegas." "Like what—legal prostitution?" Alex adds. Incredulous, Isabel reacts, "That is such a guy thing to say". Lanie admits that she did not like Vegas initially, but it has grown on her, but Jeff adds, "Vegas is a sandbox. A sandbox for adults with too much money. New York is New York. You got culture, you got museums, you got the Yankees for Christ's sake." Lanie questions, "Why does every guy from New York think there's nothing west of the Hudson [River]?" Jeff begins, "How come every girl from Vegas," but Lanie tells him to shut up. The scene ends when Lanie says, "You see? This is the kind of conversation that usually happens on the second date."

Elapsed time: This scene begins at 00:41:08 and ends at 00:44:01 (DVD Scene 13)
Rating: PG-13 for sensuality and brief language
Citation: *Fools Rush In* (Columbia Pictures, 1997) screenplay written by Katherine Reback, directed by Andy Tennant

Forrest Gump   **DISCRIMINATION**
Follow dim-witted everyman, Forrest Gump (Tom Hanks) as he grows up from a small Southern town in Alabama to one of the richest men in the country. Along the way he becomes a decorated war hero, Olympic champion, civil rights activist, and more. His lifelong love for his childhood sweetheart keeps him sane in even the most trying times.

It is the first day of school and Forrest enters the school bus, but many of the children refuse to allow Forrest to sit with them; some said that the available seat was taken. Forrest narrates about the first time he met Jenny, a young girl who gave Forrest the seat next to her. Jenny asks about the braces on Forrest's legs, and Forrest explains the nature of his disability. He narrates how Jenny came to be his best friend, "Next to Mama, no one ever talked to me or asked me questions." Jenny ponders, "Are you stupid or something?" Forrest responds, "Mama says, stupid is as stupid does." The scene ends when Forrest narrates, "Me and Jenny was like peas and carrots."

Elapsed time: This scene begins at 00:12:24 and ends at 00:00:14:41 (DVD Scene 3)
Rating: PG-13 for drug content, some sensuality and war violence
Citation: *Forrest Gump* (Paramount Pictures, 1994), screenplay written by Eric Roth, directed by Robert Zemeckis

For Richer or Poorer   **DIFFERENCE/ETHNOCENTRISM**

On the run from the IRS for tax fraud, New York socialites Brad and Caroline Sexton (Tim Allen & Kirstie Alley) find themselves hiding in an old-order Amish community (in the disguise of "cousins" Jacob and Emma Yoder). Can they blend in without destroying the Amish way of life and exposing their little secret?

Jacob and Emma (Allen & Alley) are being shown to their room by their "cousin" Luvinia Yoder, who is explaining the available amenities (outhouse in the back of the house). Emma asks to use the phone; gasping, Luvinia states, "My, you must come from a liberal ordnung. Ours is one of the last remaining Old Order Amish communities in the country. We still do not receive any electricity or public works. We like to maintain our purity and independence from the government. We find it best to remain disconnected from the outside world where corruption and materialism are so commonplace." After Luvinia leaves the room, Emma (Caroline) complains: "I can't stay here. They don't have television, and they don't even have indoor plumbing, for God sakes." Jacob (Brad) chastises, "What did you expect? Room service and a Jacuzzi? It's either this or sleeping on cow pies." She returns, "Great! Cow dung or ordung." Correcting her, Jacob says, "Ordnung. Ordnung. Learn it."

Elapsed time: This scene begins at 00:38:39 and ends at 00:40:30 (DVD Scene 11)
Rating: PG-13 for some sexual innuendo and one use of strong language
Citation: *For Richer or Poorer* (Universal Pictures, 1997) written by Jana Howington & Steve Lukanic, directed by Bryan Spicer

Freedom Writers   **CO-OPTATION/STEREOTYPE**

Ms. Erin Gruwell (Hillary Swank) takes her first job as a teacher in a predominantly Black and Latino school that is impoverished. The students wage daily wars just to survive against drive-by shootings and gang warfare. She teaches the students to channel their anger, fears, and frustration through writing to give them a "voice of their own." Based upon the acclaimed best-seller, The Freedom Writers Diary.

This scene opens upon Mr. Brian Gelford's distinguished scholars honors class who has been assigned to read Alice Walker's classic *The Color Purple*. As Gelford introduces the book and writes the title on the blackboard, he states, "I thought it would be most valuable to begin with Victoria to give us the black perspective." Victoria is the only African American in the class, and she reacts starkly to Gelford's request. Internally, she says, "Do I have a stamp on my forehead that says 'The National Spokesperson for the Plight of Black People?' How the hell should I know the black perspective on *The Color Purple?*" She continues, "Teachers treat me like I'm some kind of Rosetta Stone for African Americans. What? Black people learn how to read, and we all miraculously come to the same conclusion?" The scene ends when Victoria and the others enter Ms. Gruwell's classroom.

Elapsed time: This scene begins at 01:09:00 and ends at 01:10:00 (DVD Scene 10)
Rating: PG-13 for violent content, some thematic material, and language
Citation: *Freedom Writers* (Paramount Pictures, 2007), written and directed by Richard Lagravenese

GI Jane   **SEXISM/COMPULSORY HETEROSEXUALITY**
After years of being rejected, Lt. Jordan O'Neil (Demi Moore) has finally been accepted into the training camp to be one of the elite Navy SEALS; that is, if she can make it through the hellacious training program. To be the first female SEAL, Jordan will have to take on the toughest soldiers who are intent on keeping their ranks males only.

Jordan (Moore) has been summoned to the office of Congresswoman DeHaven (Anne Bancroft) where she is notified of her acceptance into the SEALS program. DeHaven admits, "It's just a test case, Jordan, but if things work out—if you can go the distance—it could well change the military's official policy on women in combat. Or, actually, its official non-policy." Jordan tells DeHaven about being "pissed off" by one previous rejection where she was told "submarines had no bathroom facilities for women." DeHaven questions Jordan about her love life: "Have you got a man? Fiancé. Steady beau. You know, some kind of solid heterosexual? I hate asking, but I don't want this thing blowing up in our faces if you happen to be batting for the other side." Jordan blushes and admits "There's someone." The scene closes as DeHaven smiles and states, "Well, wonderful."

Elapsed time: This scene begins at 00:09:36 and ends at 00:11:37 (DVD Scene 3)
Rating: R for language and combat violence
Citation: *GI Jane* (Caravan Pictures, 1997) screenplay written by David Twohy, directed by Ridley Scott

Gangs of New York   **DISCRIMINATION/ETHNOCENTRISM**
In 1863 the five boroughs of New York were divided into ethnic enclaves; young Amsterdam Vallon (Leonardo DiCaprio) returns to the town in search of his father's killer, Bill "the Butcher" Cutting. The waves of Irish immigration into New York set the backdrop for this northern civil war of sorts.

The scene opens with a celebration announcing the abolition of the slave trade in the American states after the Civil War. Amsterdam (Leonardo DiCaprio) narrates, "In the second year of the Great Civil War, when the Irish brigade marched through the streets, New York was a city full of tribes, war chiefs, rich and poor." As he is speaking, you can hear the protests of several men who yell, "Down with Lincoln," and "Lincoln will make all white men slaves." Another man chides the marching soldiers, "That's the spirit boys. Go on off and die for your blackie friends." One of the protesters screams, "He [Lincoln] is trying to say we are no different than niggers." Amsterdam continues to talk about the immigration of the Irish (a newspaper calls them "locusts") and we see scores of people coming off ships from Ireland. Amsterdam adds, "When the Irish came, the city was in a fever.

And they got a right warm welcome." (A man screams, "Go back to Ireland, you dumb Micks!" and throws a rock in the face of an elderly woman. Someone yells, "You remember that, you bog Irish gyps!" Still another, "Get back on the boat, Paddy!") Amsterdam shares that while he had only travelled two hours from the town of Hellgate, he was mistaken for an immigrant. He says, "There were a thousand different accents in New York, and to the natives, you see, it was all the same." The scene ends when a protester yells, "America is for Americans!"

Elapsed time: This scene begins at 00:16:20 and ends at 00:00:18:25 (DVD Scene 2)
Rating: R for intense strong violence, sexuality/nudity and language
Citation: *Gangs of New York* (Miramax Films, 2003), screenplay by Jay Cocks, Steven Zallian, & Kenneth Lonergam, directed by Martin Scorcese

Glory ETHNOCENTRISM/RACISM/POWER
Robert Gould Shaw (played by Matthew Broderick) leads the US Civil War's first all-black volunteer company, fighting prejudices of both his own Union army and the Confederates. The story is drafted from a collection of the actual letters written by Captain Shaw.

Captain Shaw and his commanding officer have led their squadron to Darien, Georgia, a town where it is rumored that secessionists live. One of the soldiers (played by Morgan Freeman) announces to the leaders that there are no rebel soldiers in the town, just some women. The soldiers are ordered to pillage and set fire to the town, "Liberating it for the Republic," the colonel called it. Soon, a man comes running out of his home screaming, "Don't shoot, we ain't secess here." Captain Shaw argues that the man is a civilian and the colonel retorts, "That man is a Secess and Secess is all the same, son." Colonel mentions that the Negro soldiers are not worthy of seeing combat. He refers to them as "monkey children" and cautions Shaw that he "learns how to control them." Screams interrupt their conversation as a Negro woman tries to stop a soldier from taking the silver from her mistress. The soldier hits the servant girl and then her white mistress. Colonel tells the soldier, "Hey boy, take your hands off the white lady." The colonel shoots the soldier. He turned to Shaw and says, "Now that would not have been necessary if that secess woman hadn't started it. You see, Secess has got to be swept away by the hand of God like the Jews of old. And now I will have to burn this town." The scene ends as the men carry out the spoils from the town.

Elapsed time: This scene begins at 01:05:35 and ends at 01:09:25 (DVD Scene 19)
Rating: R for language and war-related action
Citation: *Glory* (Tristar Pictures, 1989), screenplay written by Kevin Jarre, directed by Edward Zwick

A Good Woman ETHNOCENTRISM
Few women trust their men around Mrs. Erlynne (Helen Hunt); she is known as a bit of a gold-digging tramp with a secret identity. Erlynne saves Lady Windemere

(Scarlet Johannson) from certain disgrace when she confesses to a "crime" she did not commit.

Contessa Luchino (Milena Vukotic) is walking her dogs and complaining about pain in her back as she approaches Lord Darlington (Stephen Cambell Moore) and Tuppy (Tom Wilkinson). She turns her complaints to the concern of "Americans everywhere." She laments, "You'd never know there was a depression in that country. They don't shop; they pillage! And they speak loudly. Could the entire nation be hard of hearing? Something in the diet, perhaps?" Her daughter chimes in, "But we have American friends, mama." The countess answers, "Well, they don't need to know what we say about them, dear." Lord Darlington comments, "I like America. Name me another society that's come from barbarism to decadence without bothering to create a civilization in between." Tuppy adds, "A tribute to American efficiency."

Elapsed time: This scene begins at 00:13:38 and ends at 00:14:25 (DVD Scene 4)
Rating: PG for thematic material, sensuality, and language
Citation: *A Good Woman* (Beyond Films, 2004) screenplay written by Howard Himelstein, directed by Mike Barker

The Great Debaters   SOCIAL JUSTICE
Academy Award winning actor Denzel Washington directs this biopic on the first African American debate team who sparred against Harvard University. Washington stars as Melvin Tolson, debate professor at Wiley College, who teaches his students how to effectively argue points and counterpoints while facing significant racial backlash.

The debate team from Wiley College is preparing for a historical debate with the team from Oklahoma State University—the subject for discussion is integration of colleges and universities. The Negro team from Wiley is arguing the affirmative, and Miss Booke is the first speaker. The teams argue back and forth and Miss Booke (Jurnee Smollett) and her teammate intend to prove the unconstitutionality and unfairness of segregated schools. She argues that "The Negro people are not just a color of the American fabric. They are the threads that hold it together." Their opponents cite W.E.B. DuBois, the first African American to receive a doctorate from Harvard University (and any other school in the country) who argued that Negro students would be unhappy at integrated schools and therefore unsuccessful. Another student from OSU admits "It is true. Far too many whites are afflicted with the disease of racial hatred." He continues to argue that someday in the future there will be integrated campuses, but "sadly, that day is not today." Miss Booke refutes by saying "As long as schools are segregated, Negroes will receive an education that is both separate and unequal. . . but my opponent says today is not the day for whites and colored to go to the same college, to share the same campus, to walk in the same classroom. Well, would you kindly tell me when is that day gonna come? Is it gonna come tomorrow? Is it gonna come next week?

In a hundred years? Never? No, the time for justice, the time for freedom, and the time for equality is always, is always, right now!"

Elapsed time: This scene begins at 00:53:03 and ends at 00:57:40 (DVD Scene 12)
Rating: PG-13 for depiction of strong thematic material including violence and disturbing images, and for language and brief sexuality
Citation: *The Great Debaters* (The Weinstein Company, 2007), screenplay written by Robert Eisele, directed by Denzel Washington

Guess Who's Coming to Dinner   POWER

The classic film featuring the acting talent of Spencer Tracy (in his final role), Katherine Hepburn, and Sidney Poitier. Matt and Christina (Tracy and Hepburn) learn that their daughter Joanna has met a handsome doctor and has decided to get married after a brief 10-day courtship; the excitement wanes when they learn the good doctor is black. His parents are none too thrilled about the nuptials either. Can true love last the barriers of the color line?

Christina (Katherine Hepburn) is on the terrace talking with her husband and the monsignor when her daughter, Joanna (Katharine Houghton) interrupts to tell her that Hilary has arrived and would like to speak with her. When Christina enters the living room, Hilary is speaking with Dr. John Prentice (Sideny Poitier), who is Joanna's fiancé. Joanna tells Hilary that she is going to be getting married to John; Hilary is surprised by this news that Joanna will marry a black man. Hilary works for Christina at the local art gallery and Christina wonders why Hilary has driven so far to their home; Hilary portends that it has something to do with the gallery. Christina escorts Hilary outside; once there, Hilary expresses sympathy to Christina, "My poor dear, what a shock for you. Whatever are you going to do about it?" She continues, "It's so unlike Joey (Joanna) to do anything so appallingly stupid. Oh, what you must be going through." Christina directs Hilary to get in her car, stating, "Now I have some instructions for you. I want you to go straight back to the gallery. Start your motor. When you go back to the gallery, tell Jennifer she will be looking after things temporarily. She's to give me a ring if there's anything she can't do for herself. Then go into the office and make out a check for cash for the sum of $5000. Then carefully remove absolutely everything that might subsequently remind me that you had ever been there including that yellow thing with the blue bulbs which you have such an affection for. Then take the check for $5000 which I feel you deserve and get permanently lost. It's not that I don't want to know you, although I don't. It's just that I'm afraid we're not really the sort of people that you can afford to be associated with." Hilary tries to speak, but she is preempted by Christina: "Don't speak, just go." The scene ends as Hilary drives away.

Elapsed time: This scene begins at 00:47:28 and ends at 00:50:20 (DVD Scene 12)
Rating: NR
Citation: *Guess Who's Coming to Dinner?* (Columbia Pictures, 1967) written by William Rose, directed by Stanley Kramer

CHAPTER 4

Hairspray   POWER

Tracy Turnblad has a big personality and bigger hair to match! Her life's ambition is to be a dancer on the televised "Corny Collins Show," which is against her reclusive mother's (played by John Travolta) wishes and those of the show's producer, who also happens to be the mother of her biggest rival. Tracy auditions and becomes an overnight sensation, and uses her celebrity to fight for racial integration on the primetime show.

The dancers for *The Corny Collins Show* are ending an on-camera dance; Corny signs off to commercial by announcing "We will be right back with more of that Detroit sound." The show's producer, Velma van Tussle (Michelle Pfeiffer) complains about his choice of words: "Detroit sound? What's that? The cries of people getting mugged?" Corny replies that the kids prefer R&B music, and Velma states, "They're kids, Corny. We have to steer them in the white direction." Velma's daughter, Amber (Brittany Snow), is kissing her boyfriend, Link (Zac Efron), and Velma tells her to "save your personal life for the camera, sweetie" and turns to the camera man and cries, "If you would do your job, my daughter would not have to fight to be visible." The cameraman argues "I have to show some of the other kids once in a while." Velma returns, "You know, this is a small city. They aren't that many stations. This time next year you could be wearing an ill-fitting tux and snapping bar mitzvah photos." The scene ends when Velma walks away.

Elapsed time: This scene begins at 00:11:35 and ends at 00:13:07 (DVD Scene 3)
Rating: PG for language, some suggestive content, and momentary teen smoking
Citation: *Hairspray* (New Line Cinema, 2007), written by Leslie Dixon, directed by Adam Shankman

Hamlet 2   PREJUDICE

Dana Marchsz is an actor and playwright searching for a hit show, but his career has stalled (flopped) and he has become a volunteer high school drama teacher. He and his students stage an original update of Shakespeare's classic without all of the tragedy.

Dana Marchsz (Steve Coogan) is rehearsing with his drama class when Octavio (whom Marchsz refers to as Heywood) arrives late. Octavio, a Latino teenager, informs his teacher that his father no longer allows him to participate as the lead in the school's play. Marchsz assumes some cultural rules at play and screams, "Goddamn macho bastards and their fear of the arts! They just don't get it." He composes himself and declares, "OK, we're fighting this—even if we have to take on the whole ghetto." Despite Octavio's objections, Marchsz goes to see his parents to discuss this matter. Speaking to Octavio's father, Marchsz states, "You can't let your ethnic narrow-mindedness stop your son from thriving in our culture." Octavio's dad objects, "I have to take exception to that characterization." Marchsz states, "Heywood's a bad boy, a gang banger, a deadbeat. But he also has a gift." The parents question, "Who's Heywood?" On the first day of class, Octavia told Marchsz that his name was Heywood Jablomey. Octavio's dad corrects

Marchsz's conclusions about his son: "Octavio does not belong to a gang. He's got a 3.9 and an early acceptance to Brown [University]." He continues by citing his objections to the play as simply being an "absolute distaste for a sequel to what is arguably the greatest play in the English language. Not to mention the quality of the writing, which is quite low [Marchsz wrote the play]." Offended, Marchsz scoffs, "Well, no offense, but what the hockey puck do you know?" Octavio's father cites his credentials: "Well, I've published nine novels. I have a PhD in literature. My wife is a painter. She currently has an exhibit at the Guggenheim in Bilbao." The scene ends as the parents consent to allowing Octavio to make up his own mind and Marchsz leaves.

Elapsed time: This scene begins at 00:37:54 and ends at 00:40:50 (DVD Scene 8)
Rating: R for language including sexual references, brief nudity and some drug content
Citation: *Hamlet 2* (Focus Features, 2008) written by Pam Brady & Andrew Fleming, directed by Andrew Fleming

Happy Feet   DIFFERENCE
Mumble, the young penguin, faces the ire of his entire village of emperor penguins. All of the other penguins love to sing, but not Mumble, he is a dancer. When he is kicked out of Emperor Land, Mumble sets out on a journey to prove the importance of being true to yourself.

All of the other penguins have seen the birth of their young hatchlings, but Memphis's egg is yet to hatch. As this scene begins, the egg begins to crack and the father could not be any prouder—that is, until the young chick comes out of the egg. Before we see his face, the hatching's feet pop out and he begins waddling along; Memphis declares, "That's different." The elder penguins notice the funny way Mumble walks and question, "What do you make of that? Little wobbly in the knees. Is he okay?" Memphis asks his son, "What you doing there, boy?" Mumble answers, "I'm just happy, Pa." Memphis wonders, "What you doing with your feet, boy?" When Mumble mentions that he has happy feet, Memphis cautions him, "I wouldn't do that around folks, son. It just ain't penguin." Later all of the penguin men greet the women when they return from hunting; the mothers are anxious to greet their newborn children. When Mumble's mom notices how her child walks, she questions, "Hey, what's wrong with his feet?" Memphis remarks, "Oh that's just a little thing he's got going there. He'll grow out of it." Later, in school the students learn how to sing their heartsongs, the method of finding a life mate. The teacher adds, "Without our heartsongs, we can't be truly penguin, can we?" Several students sing their heartsongs, and they are followed by Mumble who lets out a loud screech. The elders question who let out the noise and one states, "That is the offspring of Memphis and Norma Jean: the wee hippity hopper." The other penguins laugh at Mumble and one argues, "A penguin without a heartsong is hardly a penguin at all." The elder penguins discuss a possible cause for Mumble's disability, including problems during incubation. Mumble's parents take him to see a voice coach; he ultimately fails singing but begins to dance around happily.

Norma Jean questions, "So he's a little different. I always kinda liked different." Memphis argues, "He's not different. He's a regular emperor penguin." The scene ends when Memphis urges Mumble to try to learn how to sing.

Elapsed time: This scene begins at 00:07:37 and ends at 00:18:00 (DVD Scene 3)
Rating: G for all audiences
Citation: *Happy Feet* (Kingdom Feature Productions, 2006), written by John Colle and Warren Coleman, directed by George Miller and Warren Coleman

Harold & Kumar Escape from Guantanamo Bay   RACISM/DISCRIMINATION
On the morning after their White Castle run, potheads Harold Lee (John Cho) and Kumar Patel (Kal Penn) return, and in this installment, are on a cross country adventure to prove they are not terrorists after they were arrested for trying to bring a bong (drug paraphernalia) on an airplane. They find themselves as the "guests" of the American government at the prison on Guantanamo Bay, Cuba.

Harold and Kumar have just escaped from Guantanamo Bay in Cuba and have borrowed a car from a friend in Miami. They are en route to Texas to see a friend who works for the federal government. During their conversation, they question how the news of the arrest will affect their parents. The scene flashes to their parents being interviewed by members of the Department of Homeland Security. Kumar's father reacts negatively to his son's arrest and the agent responds, "You Arabs think you can just mix in with our peaceful society and we're not going to find you, huh?" Mr. Patel argues "I am not Arab! I am Indian!" The agent turns to a translator and asks him to speak to Harold's parents about Harold's supposed terrorist activity (even though the Lees speak perfect English and do not need a translator). Mr. Lee mentions that his family has been citizens for over 40 years and he finds this maltreatment offensive. The translator turns to the agent and states, "They're using some sort of dialect I've never heard before, but I am pretty sure he said something about going on the offensive." Mr. Patel and Mrs. Lee argue that their sons are upstanding citizens; Kumar is "supposed to be in medical school" and the agent yells, "They are supposed to be in prison. That is where terrorists belong." He threatens to catch the fugitives dead or alive, and tells the translator, "Tell them that in your fake ching-chong language" and exits the room.

Elapsed time: This scene begins at 00:28:14 and ends at 00:30:19 (DVD Scene 7)
Rating: R for strong, crude, and sexual content, graphic nudity, pervasive language and drug use
Citation: *Harold & Kumar Escape from Guantanamo Bay* (New Line Cinemas, 2008) written and directed by Jon Hurwitz and Hayden Schlossberg

Head of State   **CO-OPTATION**
In an oddly prophetic tale of the first African American to be elected president of the United States through a grassroots, community organizing platform, Mays Gilliam (Chris Rock) earns the trust of party leaders and the general public as he

promises to take care of the needs of the people of the country rather than needs of big government.

The two candidates for the office of president of the United States have been killed in a plane crash and the party officials are trying to decide the person they will nominate to face the incumbent. Senator Bill Arnot (James Rebhorn) is leading the initiative to replace the nominees; although he believes that there is no real possibility for the next candidate to actually win. He argues that the goal for the election is to "set the party up for the next election" [which he plans to run for]. Instead, he argues, the party needs "a candidate who will put on a good show." Campaign manager Debra Lassiter (Lynn Whitfield) questions "Who will run a race they know they can't win?" Arnot responds, "Who says he has to know?" The scene cuts to their choice, Mays Gilliam (Chris Rock) who is local alderman in Washington, DC. In a later meeting, Arnot, Lassiter, and Martin Geller (Dylan Baker) who are assessing the value of having a Black candidate run for the highest office; Arnot mentions, "I think we found our man. This is America, see? Little guy against the big guy, corporations against the people, young versus old. What's better than this?" Lassiter questions how Gilliam can help the party; Arnot responds, "The United States is changing. America is changing. Inside of twenty years, you know the numbers: 20% black, 21% Asian, 39% Hispanic—the minorities will be the majority. The smartest thing we can do is be the first party to nominate a minority for president." Another congressman asks, "How about a cripple?" Arnot continues, "Now, we'll lose, of course, but the minorities will be happy. The minorities will be happy and they will vote for us in 2008 because we've shown them we support them; and the white guys will vote for us because our guy isn't black." The unnamed congressman responds, "You got my vote!" The scene ends when Arnot promises that once he is president he will take care of Lassiter.

Elapsed time: This scene begins at 00:09:12 and ends at 00:13:08 (DVD Scene 3)
Rating: PG-13 for language, some sexuality and drug references
Citation: *Head of State* (Dreamworks Pictures, 2003) written by Chris Rock & Ali LeRoi, directed by Chris Rock

Heavyweights   OUT-GROUP
A camp for overweight kids is bought out by a fitness guru wannabe who will stop at nothing to turn his charges into lean, mean, fighting machines. The campers have no desire to exercise all summer, so they stage a mutiny to take back their beloved Camp Hope.

Pat (Tom McKinley), a defrocked counselor, is sitting on the deck by the lake when he is joined by a camper named Gerry (Aaron Schwartz). Pat has been watching the activities of the athletic MVP camp across the lake from his "fat camp." Pat confides to Gerry, "I wonder what it would feel like to be one of those guys. Just once I want to score a winning touchdown." He reflects on the fact that he had never scored a point in any game he has played. "I'm just so tired of being the fat guy," Pat continues. Gerry empathetically responds, "I know; but you don't want to be one of those guys. They're jerks. Forget them." Pat and Gerry begin yelling defiantly across the lake, "Keep your washboard stomachs and oily muscles. I don't want them!" Sadly, Pat returns, "I'm still tired of being the fat guy." Their conversations turns to talking about how the owner of the camp, Tony Perkis (Ben Stiller), had earlier in the day embarrassed them for being overweight. Gerry tries to comfort Pat saying, "At least you stood up to him. Nobody else had the guts to. We should've backed you up. When are we going to start sticking up for ourselves?" The two begin to plot how they can teach Tony a lesson. Pat tells Gerry to rally the troops saying, "He is one. We are many." The scene ends when the conspirators slap high five.

Elapsed time: This scene begins at 00:56:52 and ends at 00:59:11 (DVD Scene 8)
Rating: PG for some rude language and pranks
Citation: *Heavyweights* (Walt Disney Pictures, 1995) written by Judd Apatow & Steven Brill, directed by Steven Brill

Higher Learning   **OUT-GROUP/ PREJUDICE**
Director John Singleton weaves an interlocking tale of the struggles of freshman year at fictional Columbus University—dealing with diversity, identity, and belonging. Malik (Omar Epps) is a new student at Columbus and he is quickly overwhelmed by the collegiate life. He and his roommate are from differing backgrounds, his professor (Laurence Fishburne) rides him, and race relations are at an all-time low.

Malik (Epps) and Professor Phipps (Fishburne) are having a discussion about Malik's initial adjustment to college life. Malik explains how he feels that, as an African-American, he faces mental prejudice and that he must outperform his White peers. Malik says, "I got a problem with the way these fools be trippin' when they see a black face." Phipps asks, "Did someone spit in your face when you first came to campus? Was there a cross burned outside your dormitory?" Malik argues, "No, and I know what you're trying to get at. Look man, just cause it ain't up in my face, don't mean it ain't happening. It's less physical now, more mental. I gotta run and study man. I don't see these white folks worrying about nothing but going to class and playing handball, talking about skiing and all. They don't have the same worries I do." Dr. Phipps explains that Malik's problems are not racial, but economic and financial. Phipps begins to lay out a scenario for Malik: "You are a runner, are you not?" Malik argues that he is one of the best. Phipps adds, "Let's just say, for instance, you are running a race and you suspect the opposing team has a member who is faster, stronger, more big time than yourself. What do you do then? Do you leave the track? What do you do?" Malik stridently scoffs, "Run faster." Phipps smiles and the scene cuts to Malik sitting at his desk reading one of his textbooks well into the night.

Elapsed time: This scene begins at 01:01:56 and ends at 01:04:02 (DVD Scene 13)
Rating: R for sexual violence and strong language

Citation: *Higher Learning* (Columbia Pictures, 1994), written and directed by John Singleton

Higher Learning   SEXISM/DISCRIMINATION
Director John Singleton weaves an interlocking tale of the struggles of freshman year at fictional Columbus University—dealing with diversity, identity, and belonging. Malik (Omar Epps) is a new student at Columbus and he is quickly overwhelmed by the collegiate life. He and his roommate are from differing backgrounds, his professor (Laurence Fishburne) rides him, and race relations are at an all-time low.

Kristen (Kristy Swanson) is passing out flyers for Students for a Non-Sexist Society, a women's group that discusses issues of sexuality and safety and security. A male named Wayne asks Kristen for a flyer, but she refuses and says that the group is only open to women; Wayne challenges this as contradictory: "You want a non-sexist society, but you won't give me a flyer because I'm a man? That's not cool." Kristen wonders, "Well, why do you really want to come?" The scene ends as Wayne compliments her new hair style.

Elapsed time: This scene begins at 01:05:00 and ends at 01:05:54 (DVD Scene 13)
Rating: R for sexual violence and strong language
Citation: *Higher Learning* (Columbia Pictures, 1994), written and directed by John Singleton

The Hot Chick   COMPULSORY HETEROSEXUALITY
Jessica (Rachel McAdams) is the queen of the high school totem pole, and she makes sure everyone knows it. When she purchases cursed earrings at a local store, she mystically trades bodies with a ne'er-do-well named Spencer (Rob Schneider). As Spence, she learns what people really think of her.

April (Anna Farris) and Jessica (in the body of Spence; played by Rob Schneider) are attending the high school prom where they have plans to attempt to make April's ex-boyfriend, Jake, jealous by kissing in front of him and his prom date. What Jessica/Spence does not know is that April has fallen in love with her/him. April admits, "I don't really care about Jake anymore. There's no one I'd rather be here with tonight. April and Jessica/Spence each express their gratitude to the other for their lifelong friendship. Spence tells April, "Any guy would be lucky to have you; and I should know. I've been a guy for almost a week now; and in that time you have been such a good friend to me. I don't know how I could ever thank you." April and Spence kiss as Jake is walking by after which Spence declares, "I am so lesbian right now." Jake clearly disapproves of the kiss and storms away. April tries to kiss Spence again, but Spence rebuffs her saying, "We already got him, honey. He can't see us anymore." April declares her love for Spence, adding "You're my best friend, and now you're a guy. It's meant to be." Spence wonders, We're not gonna let a little thing like me turning into a man and you wanting to be with me get in the way of our friendship are we?" From a distance, Spence sees her boyfriend,

Billy, and declares her love for him. "If I'm going to be stuck like this forever," Jessica/Spence pines, "he's just going to have to accept me as I am—a man." Billy is with his own prom date and soon Spence head butts her so that she can talk with Billy. Spence admits that he is really Jessica; he attempts to convince Billy by describing various intimate moments the two have shared. Spence tells Billy to close his eyes, and Spence tries to kiss him; Billy rejects him/her. Spence pleads, "You always said you'd love me no matter what!" Before he runs away, Billy cries, "But—I—you're a thirty year old dude!"

Elapsed time: This scene begins at 01:22:18 and ends at 01:28:42 (DVD Scene 10)
Rating: PG-13 on appeal for crude and sexual humor, language and drug references
Citation: *The Hot Chick* (Touchstone Pictures, 2002) written by Tom Brady & Rob Schneider, directed by Tom Brady

Hotel Rwanda   ETHNOCENTRISM/RACISM
Paul Rusesabinga (Paul Cheadle) finds himself an unlikely champion as he is forced to house and protect hundreds of people in the hotel he manages. The refugees are fleeing the civil strife in Rwanda as war ravages the country. Based on a true story.

Paul (Cheadle) is speaking alone with Colonel Oliver (Nick Nolte) who is commanding the Western relief efforts. Paul congratulates Oliver on performing well, but Oliver responds, "You should spit in my face." Paul is confused by this statement and Oliver continues, "You're dirt. We think you're dirt, Paul." Paul asks, "Who is 'we?'" Oliver coldly responds, "The west—all the superpowers—everything you believe in, Paul. They think you're dirt. They think you're dung. You're worthless." He compliments Paul, "You could own this freakin' hotel; except for one thing…you're black. You're not even a nigger. You're African." The scene ends when Colonel Oliver tells Paul that the soldiers are not going to protect them by stopping the slaughter.

Elapsed time: This scene begins at 00:49:20 and ends at 00:50:45 (DVD Scene 12)
Rating: PG-13 on appeal for violence, disturbing images and brief strong language
Citation: *Hotel Rwanda* (United Artists, 2004) written by Keir Pearson & Terry George, directed by Terry George

I am Legend   PRIVILEGE
What would it like to be the last man standing in all of New York City (and possibly the world)? Colonel Robert Neville (Will Smith) is left on his own to find an antidote for a virus that is ravaging the city and turning its survivors into bloodthirsty mutants who wander in the darkness. Somehow immune to the virus, Neville must race against the clock before he becomes one of the hunted.

Colonel Neville and his family are attempting to flee the city, but are finding it difficult to pass the throngs of people who are doing the same. A soldier gives the command to "Keep the colonel and his family between us and don't let anyone stop you." As they force themselves through the crowds, a voice over a loudspeaker states

"Unless you have clearance, you cannot pass the checkpoint. Please return to your homes." When they reach the gated checkpoint, all citizens must be scanned for signs of infection; infected persons are forbidden access. Colonel Neville and his daughter are cleared, when a woman behind a barricade pleads for Neville to take her baby; the woman is told to move back. Neville's wife Zoe, however, does not pass the scanning and is initially barred. Using his military rank, Neville orders the lieutenant to scan his wife again; she passes the second test and is admitted to the waiting helicopter. The woman again pleads for Neville to take her baby with them. Neville's daughter questions, "Daddy, why can't the little girl come too?" Neville does not respond. The scene ends as Neville's family is whisked away in the helicopter.

Elapsed time: This scene begins at 00:39:13 and ends at 00:44:03 (DVD Scene 12)
Rating: PG 13 for intense sequences of sci-fi action and violence
Citation: *I am Legend* (Warner Bros. Pictures, 2007) written by Mark Protosevich & Akiva Goldsman, directed by Francis Lawrence

I am Sam   DIFFERENCE
Sam (played by Sean Penn) tries to raise his daughter young daughter despite the developmental delays that have left him with the IQ of a seven year old child. All is well until the Child Protective Services unit attempts to take Lucy (Dakota Fanning) away from him. Sam is desperate to prove that love, not intelligence, is the secret to being a loving father.

Sam and Lucy share tender moments every day at the park. In this scene, Lucy is inquiring about a variety of subjects by asking her dad questions such as, "Daddy, why does the snow flake?," and "Daddy, what is mustard made of?" Sam answers her in the only way his able. For instance, his answer to the mustard question was "Because it is yellow ketchup." Later, at the International House of Pancakes, Lucy raises deeper level questions about death and dying, and she wonders if her mother will ever return to the family. Getting more serious, Lucy asks, "Daddy, did God mean for you to be like this or was it an accident?" Sam questions what she means and Lucy responds, "I mean you're different. You're not like other daddies." Sam gets agitated and begins apologizing. Young Lucy attempts to calm him down by saying, "Don't be sorry. I'm lucky. No one else's daddy comes to the park." Sam responds, "Yeah, we are lucky." The scene ends as Sam cheers when his meal is served and he thanks the waitress.

Elapsed time: This scene begins at 00:12:36 and ends at 00:15:27(DVD Scene 4)
Rating: PG 13 for language
Citation: *I am Sam* (New Line Cinema, 2001) written by Kristine Johnson & Jessie Nelson, directed by Jessie Nelson

In and Out   HOMOPHOBIA/COMPULSORY HETEROSEXUALITY
Howard Brackett (Kevin Kline) is a well-liked, successful high school English teacher; that is, until a former student, while accepting an Academy Award,

announces on national television that Mr. Brackett is gay (just three days before he is scheduled to get married). A media blitz, concerned parents, and a principal add much pressure as Brackett tries to defend himself.

Several young men are sitting in the locker room discussing the recent news about Mr. Brackett; they do not believe that Brackett is gay. Another student, Mike, begins, "But think about, I mean, gay guys…there's only two times where it's OK to do gay stuff—two emergency situations—prison, when it's a substitute, or guys in space. Not on purpose. It just happens because they're weightless and they float into each other when they're asleep." He continues, "I know it's wrong; it's against, like, nature. Basic plumbing. It's the human body; it's divided up into in-holes and out-holes. Stuff is supposed to go in the in-holes and out the out-holes, but gay guys put stuff in the out-holes. Another student questions of the mouth is an in-hole, and Mike agrees "Because you put burgers in it and brew; unless you're sick and you puke, then it's an out-hole, so it's wrong." Soon Mr. Brackett (Klein) enters the locker room and the boys nervously begin to cover up and hide. Brackett questions this strange behavior, and Mike asks that Brackett leave the room until they get dressed. Brackett wonders if their actions are related to the Oscars announcement; although he says it is not, Mike mentions, "Before the Oscars, it was different. I mean, you weren't…famous." The scene ends when Brackett walks out the door.

Elapsed time: This scene begins at 00:23:48 and ends at 00:25:48 (DVD Scene 7)
Rating: PG-13 for sexual content and some strong language
Citation: *In and Out* (Paramount Pictures, 1997) written by Paul Rudnick, directed by Frank Oz

In and Out   GENDER
Howard Brackett (Kevin Kline) is a well-liked, successful high school English teacher; that is, until a former student, while accepting an Academy Award, announces on national television that Mr. Brackett is gay (just three days before he is scheduled to get married). A media blitz, concerned parents, and a principal add much pressure as Brackett tries to defend himself.

Everyone in town thinks Mr. Brackett is gay; they tell him it is because of his mannerisms, his style of dress, his neatness. In this scene, Mr. Brackett purchases an audiotape series on "Exploring Your Masculinity" where he will learn how to act like a "real man." The voice on the tape asks, "Are you dressed in suitably masculine attire?" Brackett affirms; he is wearing jeans and a flannel shirt. The announcer continues, "Are you in control? Are you ready to take charge? Are you a man?" Brackett effeminately waves his hand as says, "yes." The announcer tells him to stand up straight and tall. Brackett puts his hand on his hip and the voices asks, "Excuse me, are we a little teapot?" He tells Brackett to untuck his shirt while stating, "You want to be neat. You want to be tidy." Brackett them must pretend he's in a bar and mingling with others. Brackett must repeat several phrases, one of which "what a fabulous window treatment" was a trick. The voice skips to the "most critical element of masculine behavior—dancing." Brackett seems pleased with the subject, until the announcer states, "True manly men, do not dance—under any circumstances. While "I will Survive" plays in the background, the voice dictates, "This will be your ultimate test. At all costs avoid rhythm, grace, and pleasure. Whatever you do, do not dance." The song grows louder and Brackett cannot contain his desire to dance; the more intense the music, the more he has difficulty holding back. Soon he is dancing all over the room as the announcer shouts various insults at him including sissy, ballerina, and pussy boy. He tells Brackett to think about John Wayne or Arnold Schwarzenegger, and instead of dancing, he should "kick someone, punch someone, bite someone's ear!" The scene ends when Brackett turns off the cassette player.

Elapsed time: This scene begins at 00:42:05 and ends at 00:46:04 (DVD Scene 7)
Rating: PG-13 for sexual content and some strong language
Citation: *In and Out* (Paramount Pictures, 1997) written by Paul Rudnick, directed by Frank Oz

It's a Mad, Mad, Mad, Mad World   **ETHNOCENTRISM/GENDER**
Stanley Kramer's classic comedy follows a crew of crazed people on a statewide race to find a hidden treasure of $350,000 left by a criminal some fifteen years earlier. Along the way, the racers face a litany of obstacles, including each other. A star studded cast including: Spencer Tracy, Milton Berle, Sid Caesar, Buddy Hackett, Ethel Merman, and Mickey Rooney.

J. Russell Finch (Milton Berle) is the passenger in a car driven by a British gentleman and the two have been arguing for some time. This scene begins with the British man stating, "I've no wish to quarrel with you, but speaking as a representative of Her Majesty's armed forces, I take the most particular exception..." but is interrupted by Finch who contends, "As far as I'm concerned the whole British race is practically finished. If it we hadn't kept your whole country afloat by giving you billions you never even said 'thank you' for, the whole phony outfit would be sunk under the Atlantic years ago." The man threatens to put Finch out of the car, but Finch promptly apologizes for insulting England. The man returns, "I'm glad to hear you say so. I must say, if I had the misfortune to be a citizen of this benighted country, I should be most hesitant if offering any criticism whatever of any other!" Finch reacts, "Wait a minute! Are you knocking this country? Are you saying something against America?" The driver argues, "Against it? I'd be astounded to hear anything *for* it. The whole bloody place is the most unspeakable matriarchy in the whole history of civilization. Look at yourself—the way your wife and her strumpet of a mother push you through the hoop. As far as I can see, American men have been totally emasculated. They're like slaves. They die like flies of coronary thrombosis while their women sit under hair dryers eating chocolates and arranging for every second Tuesday to be some sort of Mother's Day. And this positively infantile pre-occupation with bosoms...in all this time in this wretched country the one thing that has appalled me most is this preposterous preoccupation with bosoms. They've become the dominant theme in American culture: in literature, in advertising, in entertainment, in everything. I'll wager you anything you like if American women stopped wearing brassieres, your whole national economy would collapse overnight."

Elapsed time: This scene begins at 01:10:20 and ends at 01:12:09 (DVD Scene 15)
Rating: G for general audiences
Citation: *It's a Mad, Mad, Mad, Mad World* (MGM, 1963) written by William Rose & Tania Rose, directed by Stanley Kramer

Jawbreaker   **CO-OPTATION**
Someone once said that the high school days are the time of one's life; but for poor Liz Purr (Charlotte Ayanna), high school is the time of her death—at the hands of her own friends. When social misfit Fern (Judy Greer) learns about the cover up of the accidental murder, she finds a way to make mutiny on the social order of the school.

As the popular girls' clique of Courtney (Rose McGowan), Marcie (Julie Benz), and Julie (Rebecca Gayheart) are trying to cover up the accidental murder of their friend Liz by staging the room to look like a rape, nerdy social misfit Fern (Judy Greer) stumbles upon the scene. When she realizes that Liz is dead, Fern runs screaming from the bedroom and the others chase her to the backyard and force her to sit down. Courtney admits their involvement in Liz's death, and is concerned that "We've got a bit of a problem, because you know we did it. You heard us. That gives you a little something, and it's called power. The power to tell. And you're the kind of girl that tells—a tattletale." Courtney continues talking to Fern, "I know all about you. You're the one in the corner at dances that the geeks won't dance with because they're at home fucking old pervs in cyberspace thinking they're doing some hot babe. There's nothing to hide Fern, you're nothing. We're everything. You're the shadow; we're the sun. But I'm here to offer you something you'd never dare dream of—something that you were never meant to be , but will be, because today, Fern, my dear, fate has decided that you are cool. We're going to make you one of us: beautiful, popular, loved, feared, all that you ever dreamed of. If, and only if, you never, ever, tell anyone what you heard. Think of it." After Julie balks of this plan to "own someone by making them beautiful," Courtney tells Fern, "Liz is dead. Take her place. You know you want it. Think about the boys." The scene ends after Fern's beauty makeover and she joins the others walking down the hallway in school.

Elapsed time: This scene begins at 00:18:55 and ends at 00:25:24 (DVD Scene 8)
Rating: R for sexuality, language and violence, all involving teens
Citation: *Jawbreaker* (Tristar Pictures, 1999) written and directed by Darren Stein

Jawbreaker   **IN-GROUP**
Someone once said that the high school days are the time of one's life; but for poor Liz Purr (Charlotte Ayanna), high school is the time of her death—at the hands of

her own friends. When social misfit Fern (Judy Greer) learns about the cover up of the accidental murder, she finds a way to make mutiny on the social order of the school.

Courtney (Rose McGowan) and Marcie (Julie Benz) are sitting at lunch with their new friend, Vylette (who is actually Fern, the former outcast in a pretty disguise). Fern/Vylette begins to open her lunch when Courtney and Marcie begin to chastise her for the act: "We never ever eat at lunch period. Do you understand me? And if for some damn good reason we did we would never ever eat from a brown paper bag." Courtney continues, "Don't think we're anorexic or something. We're not. That's reserved for the Karen Carpenter table [she points to a table of four waif-looking young women who are sharing a small box of raisins]." She explains how people will judge them by what they eat—"It gives them ammo, and the only ones with ammo are us. I would not be caught dead eating a greasy pizza, not even in front of the ultra-special students: the deaf, the dumb, and the blind because of some terrifying level they're associating that greasy pizza with your shiny face. It's just another vexing stress that we don't need." Marcie chimes in, "Life is hard enough without added anxiety." Soon Dane, a cool guy, sits down for introductions to Vylette. After he leaves, Courtney discusses why she suddenly called Fern Vylette. "It's called thinking on your toes—a must if you are going to rule the school." Courtney explains how it would be better to be a flower instead of a plant. She says, "A rose, too obvious. Never send a rose unless died black as a warning. And, if one is sent to you, destroy it, along with the sender. Emotionally, of course; it's not like we kill people...on purpose. Anyway, you're extra fancy. You're Vylette, my Vylette." The scene ends as Courtney and Vylette link hands.

Elapsed time: This scene begins at 00:27:44 and ends at 00:30:36 (DVD Scene 9)
Rating: R for sexuality, language and violence, all involving teens
Citation: *Jawbreaker* (Tristar Pictures, 1999) written and directed by Darren Stein

The Jerk   RACISM/DISCRIMINATION
Raised as a "poor Black child," Navin Johnson (Steve Martin) leaves his adopted family in the South and makes his way to the city in search of the fame and fortune. His rags to riches (and back to rags) story is a story of a man and his dog in search of love and for the music that feeds the soul.

Navin (Steve Martin) has become rich overnight because of his new invention, the Opti-Grab. Since coming into this financial windfall, numerous charities and individuals have come to him for financial assistance. In this scene, several men, who look like wise guys, are requesting $500,000 to build an upscale housing complex. The men promise to set high rental prices to keep out the "eggplants" and "jungle bunnies." Navin, who was raised by a Black family, is unfamiliar with these terms and the men explain that they are referring to "niggers." At this, Navin yells, "I am a nigger' and commences to thrash the other men" (to end the scene).

Elapsed time: This scene begins at 01:13:47 and ends at 01:15:34 (DVD Scene 13)
Rating: R for drug use, language, and violence
Citation: *The Jerk* (Universal Pictures, 1979) written by Steve Martin & Carl Gottlieb, directed by Carl Reiner

Jungle Fever   **DISCRIMINATION**
Flipper Purify (Wesley Snipes), an up-and-coming Black architect at a prestigious firm has an affair with an Italian secretary at his office. Both Angela (Annabelle Sierra) and Flipper must face the ire of their friends and family. Can their new love stand the test?

Flipper and Angela are having dinner at Sylvia's, a famous soul food restaurant in Harlem. They are refused service for a lengthy period of time. When the waitress finally asks if she can take their order, Flipper complains, "You could have taken my order 30 minutes ago when I sat my black ass in this chair." Ignoring him, the waitress interrupts and speaks coldly to Angela, "Can I take *your* order?" At that, Flipper questions, "Excuse me, do you have a problem?" The waitress (Queen Latifah) voices her frustrations with Flipper's decision to bring a White woman into the restaurant: "Yes, I do have a problem to be honest with you. Fake, tired brothers like you coming in here. That's so typical. I can't even believe you brought her stringy-haired ass up in here." Flipper returns, "First of all, let me tell you something Miss Al Sharp ton, it's not your business who I bring in here." Speaking over him, the waitress adds, "Parade your white meat somewhere else." When Flipper challenges her to do her job, the waitress begins detailing the daily specials, "Maryland crab cakes, Creole shrimp gumbo, and blackened catfish." She adds, "I suggest you have the blackened catfish." Flipper demands to see the manager, which angers the waitress. The waitress walks away and they trade final comments. Flipper screams, "You're fired" and the waitress yells, "You're tired." The scene ends as two female patrons lean close to one another and declare, "She's white" [referring to Angela].

Elapsed time: This scene begins at 00:51:53 and ends at 00:53:37 (DVD Scene 11)
Rating: R for drug use, language, and violence
Citation: *Jungle Fever* (40 Acres and a Mule Filmworks, 1991) written and directed by Spike Lee

Lakeview Terrace   **DIFFERENCE/CO-OPTATION**
A young interracial couple purchases their dream home with the hopes of starting a family and a life together. What's even better is that their next door neighbor is a veteran police officer; they feel so safe. Their dreams take a bitter turn when they learn that their new neighbor is not exactly throwing out the welcome wagon for this couple; in fact, he hopes to push them out. How do you complain to the law when the problem is the law? Samuel L. Jackson, Kerry Washington, and Patrick Wilson star.

Abel (Samuel L. Jackson) and his partner, Javier (Jay Hernandez) are on patrol when they notice some possible illegal activity. The group of youth scatter when the police arrive, but these officers are looking for a particular man named

Clarence who is among them. Clarence is actually an informant for the police. He complains about being accosted by the officers "in front of my people." Abel justifies, "This is for your benefit, man. Now it looks like you fought the law and the law won. You can go back and be the man, instead of the crank-dealing little snitch that you are." Clarence balks, "Forget the circumstance. This shit's disrespectful to a brother." Abel snidely remarks, "Brother? Clarence, we ain't brothers. We didn't even crawl out the same evolutionary pool. What are you anyway? You know, I always wondered about that. You a Euro-Mexi-Japa-Chine-Stani or what? You don't even know, do you? Ain't got a clue. You a weed, that's what you are. A junkyard weed. I'll spray your ass with some Roundup." Affronted, Clarence returns, "I'm 1/7th Cherokee, bitch!" Abel scoffs, "Yeah, and the other 93% wigger. Can you do the math on that dumb ass?" Abel presses Clarence for some information—"Give me something other than this fake-ass Vanilla Ice impression." Clarence gives them details about a shooting and then when he tries to return to his friends, Abel tells him, "You get to stay in business as long as you're useful, okay?" The scene ends after Clarence walks away.

Elapsed time: This scene begins at 00:11:33 and ends at 00:13:50 (DVD Scene 4)
Rating: PG-13 for intense thematic material, violence, sexuality, language, and some drug references
Citation: *Lakeview Terrace* (Screen Gems, 2008) screenplay written by David Lougherty & Howard Korder, directed by Neil Labute

Legally Blonde   **DISCRIMINATION**
Elle Woods (played by Reese Witherspoon) has little on her mind besides her sorority sisters, popularity, and marrying well. When her beau, Warner, is accepted to Harvard Law School, he breaks up with Elle because he feels that Elle's "type" would be a liability to his future plans. Elle enrolls in Harvard Law with the hope of gaining Warner's affection, but ends up finding herself—and, winning a high profile murder case.

Several law students have gathered in the library to form a study group. Elle approaches and questions if she can be a part of the group, which includes her ex-boyfriend Warner, and his new girlfriend, Vivian, who immediately tells Elle "Our group is full." Elle questions, "Oh, is this an RSVP thing," and is rebuffed by one of the other students—"No, it's like a smart people thing, and as Viv said, we're full." Warner suggests that the group make room for Elle, but Vivian kicks him under the table. Viv turns to Elle and says, "The answer is no." As she turns to walk away, a female student sitting at a nearby table sarcastically adds, "Hey, maybe there's, like, a sorority you could, like, join instead, like?" Elle responds, "If you had come to a rush party, I would have at least been nice to you." The student responds, "Is that before you voted against me and then called me a dyke behind my back?" Elle argues before she turns and walks away, "I don't use that word. You must have heard it from Vivian."

Elapsed time: This scene begins at 00:37:00 and ends at 00:38:08 (DVD Scene 12)
Rating: PG-13 for language and sexual references
Citation: *Legally Blonde* (Metro Goldwyn Mayer Pictures, 2001), written by Karen Lutz and Kirsten Smith, directed by Robert Luketic

Little Miss Sunshine   COMPULSORY HETEROSEXUALITY

Little Olive Hoover (Abigail Breslen in her Oscar winning role) must go on a road trip with her family to attend the finals of a beauty pageant; the problem is, her family is breaking apart at the seams. Can they survive a cross country trip all stuffed in a VW minivan?

The Hoover family is gathering for dinner; they are joined by Frank Ginsberg (Steve Carrell) who has just been released from the hospital after a suicide attempt. Young Olive Hoover (Abigail Breslin) questions how Uncle Frank was injured (his wrists are taped). Olive's mother Sheryl (Toni Colette) begins to explain that Frank was not in an accident, but tried to kill himself. Richard Hoover (Greg Kinnear) objects to the appropriateness of the conversation. Olive continues to push the issue. Frank admits that he was very unhappy; Richard interrupts citing that Frank was "sick in his head." Olive wonders why Frank was unhappy, and Frank admits that he "fell in love with someone who didn't love me back." The "someone" was a male graduate student. Olive questions, "Him? It was a boy? You fell in love with a boy? That's silly." Frank agrees, "It was silly. It was very, very, very silly."

Elapsed time: This scene begins at 00:12:34 and ends at 00:14:05 (DVD Scene 3)
Rating: R for language, some sex and drug content
Citation: *Little Miss Sunshine* (Fox Searchlight Pictures, 2006), written by Michael Arndt, directed by Jonathan Dayton and Valerie Faris

Lost in Translation   DIFFERENCE

After a series of encounters while in Japan, Bob Harris (Bill Murray), an actor who is in town to shoot a whiskey commercial, and Charlotte (Scarlett Johannson), another American, begin a friendship while they learn the customs of a foreign land.

Bob (Murray) is on the set of the Suntory whiskey commercial; the director, speaking in Japanese, gives Bon instructions on how to stage the scene. The director rambles on and on, but the interpreter gives only minimal translations. Bob seems lost and questions if the director isn't saying other things. The director seems more agitated each time Bob asks a question, and he continues to speak only in Japanese. The translator still only gives short responses that do not seem to match the director's extensive commentary.

Elapsed time: This scene begins at 00:08:31 and ends at 00:11:59 (DVD Scene 4)
Rating: R for some sexual content
Citation: *Lost in Translation* (Focus Features, 2003) written and directed by Sofia Coppola

Lords of Discipline   RACISM

One soldier must take on the age old tradition of exclusion in the ranks of a southern military institution as he protects the school's first African American cadet. Will (David Keith) learns of a group of elite soldiers who violently coerce cadets to quit the school. Can he buck a system that he was sworn to protect?

The new cadets at Carolina Military Institute are being subjected to the first days of ridicule known as Hell Week. Will (David Keith), one of the cadet leaders, and his commander are watching the activities. The commander (Robert Prosky) is scanning the melee for the sight of "fly shit in the sugar," namely Cadet Pearce (Mark Preland), the first Black cadet to enroll in the academy. Pearce is being berated by his platoon leaders who are requiring him to repeat derogatory phrases such as, "I'm an ugly black boy" and "I'm an ugly shoeshine." Commander bear remarks "He ain't here to fry chicken or mow the lawn. That Negro's joining the Long Grey Line." Bear refers to Pearce as a "pickaninny, a jigaboo, a coon—why not a plain old nigger" when referring to the names the other cadets will call Pearce. Bear asks Will to protect Pearce. Will questions Bear: "Are you a racist?" Bear admits, "Yeah, I'm a racist. I'd like nothing better than to see Mr. Pearce move his black ass right out of here." Will questions why Bear wants Pearce protected; Bear argues "because as of right now Pearce is one of my lambs, and all of my lambs get an even break." The scene ends as Pearce is continually being denigrated.

Elapsed time: This scene begins at 00:12:05 and ends at 00:15:15 (DVD Scene 2)
Rating: R for language, violence, and strong thematic issues
Citation: *Lords of Discipline* (Paramount Pictures, 1983) screenplay written by Thomas Pope & Lloyd Fonvielle, directed Frank Roddam

Lords of Discipline   IN-GROUP

One soldier must take on the age old tradition of exclusion in the ranks of a southern military institution as he protects the school's first African American cadet. Will (David Keith) learns of a group of elite soldiers who violently coerce cadets to quit the school. Can he buck a system that he was sworn to protect?

Will (David Keith) has been called to the General Durrell's office; the general questions why Will did not participate in the Hell Night activities. Will admits that he did not enjoy the activities when they were being perpetrated on him, so he could not see doing them to others. The general himself admits that he dislikes the mistreatment of the cadets; "I loathe deliberately cruelty because I'm a soldier, not a sadist. But will, you have to understand the purpose of the Institute. We are called to produce something special—almost unique—in this day and age: the whole man. The system is hard, but it's fair. And more importantly, it works." Will questions whether the system will work for Mr. Pearce, the Institute's first African American. General Durrell tells him: "for the system to work, it needs—it must have your active participation." Will interrupts, "Even in the hazing of Knobs [new recruits], sir?" Durrell responds, "Certainly in the hazing of Knobs. That's part of your duty, Will. The Institute is asking for your help." The scene ends when Will exits the general's office.

Elapsed time: This scene begins at 00:32:40 and ends at 00:35:30 (DVD Scene 3)
Rating: R for language, violence, and strong thematic issues
Citation: *Lords of Discipline* (Paramount Pictures, 1983) screenplay written by Thomas Pope & Lloyd Fonvielle, directed Frank Roddam

Madagascar: Escape 2 Africa   CLASSISM
The animal hijinx continue as Alex the Lion (voiced by Ben Stiller), Marty the Zebra (Chris Rock), Melman the Giraffe (David Schwimmer), and Gloria the Hippo (Jada Pinkett Smith) attempt to leave their island paradise to return to America. When their plane crashes in Africa, they learn to love the homeland they never knew.

Alex, Marty, Melman, and Gloria are aboard an aircraft heading back to America. Melman is walking up to the front of the plane to check on their drink order. He peeks his head into the first class cabin where King Julien and Maurice are sitting. Melman remarks at the nicer conditions in first class, and Julien immediately condescendingly rebuffs him: "Do you mind going back? This is first class. It's nothing personal; we're just better than you." Julien turns to the flight attendant and addresses him as "in-flight slave." Julien tells Melman to return to the back as he swings back into his seat next to Maurice. He laments to Maurice, "Whatever happened to the separation of the classes?" Maurice responds, "I'm sure this democracy thing is just a fad."

Elapsed time: This scene begins at 00:12:05 and ends at 00:13:04 (DVD Scene 4)
Rating: PG for some mild crude language
Citation: *Madagascar: Escape 2 Africa* (Dreamworks Pictures, 2008) written by Etan Cohen, Eric Darnell, and Tom McGrath, directed by Eric Darnell & Tom McGrath

Made of Honor   GENDER
Always a best man, but never a maid of honor—this film follows Tom Bailey (Patrick Dempsey) as he has been recruited by his best friend to be her maid of honor. What Hannah (Michelle Monaghan) does not know is that Tom himself is in love with her and will do whatever he can to steal her heart away from her fiancé. Can this playboy bachelor win the hand and heart of this woman who knows what he is really like?

It's the night before Hannah's bridal shower and Tom's duties as maid of honor include putting together all of the favors and decorations. Tom invites his friends over for their usual poker night, but unbeknownst to the gentlemen, the table is covered in wedding supplies and there is no poker until the favors are done. One guy, Dennis, rejects the idea saying "I'm not playing with baskets. It's poker night." The rest of the guys really get into the task and soon are comparing candle scents over the sound of "It's Ladies' Night" playing in the background. Dennis does not participate and when invited to "come and curl some ribbon," he says, "I can feel my sperm dying inside of me one at a time. I'm going to the strip club to eat some meat. Then I'm gonna get into a fight." Before he leaves, he tells Tom to "Call me when you find your balls." One of the other guy's yells to Dennis, "Someone's afraid of his feminine side."

Elapsed time: This scene begins at 00:47:05 and ends at 00:48:30 (DVD Scene 12)
Rating: PG-13 for sexual content and language
Citation: *Made of Honor* (Columbia Pictures, 2008) screenplay written by Adam Sztykiel, Deborah Kaplan, & Harry Elfont, directed by Paul Weiland

Tyler Perry's Madea's Family Reunion   IN-GROUP/OUT-GROUP

A wedding and a family reunion in the same weekend is only a recipe for arguments and family fights, and this film has plenty of both. Join Madea (Perry) as she doles out advice and wisdom on life and love to Vanessa and Lisa, two sisters who are having issues with their men.

Vanessa and her sister Lisa have different fathers, but the same mother, who prefers Lisa to Vanessa. Lisa has escaped her abusive fiancé and her mother (Lynn Whitfield) has come to retrieve Lisa and take her back to him. Vanessa tells her mother, Victoria, that Lisa does not want to go back to Carlos. Victoria questions Lisa, "Is this how you want to live? Pathetic like your sister? Look how she lives. Is this what you want?" Vanessa reveals the secret that Victoria has been spending Lisa's trust fund, and now that it is low, she wants Lisa to marry Carlos for his money. Vanessa and Victoria are clearly estranged, and Vanessa begins to tell a story about how Victoria gave Lisa's father permission to rape Vanessa so that he would not abandon the family. At first, Lisa refuses to believe that her father was a child molester, that is, until Victoria admits, "He was going to leave. I had done everything I could in our family, everything I could to please him. If we were going to be comfortable [financially] I had to make somone hard, hard decisions." She tells Vanessa, "You should be happy you were able to save our family...Sweetheart, you were my only option." Victoria defends her actions by describing how her own mother was a prostitute and drug addict and how she allowed her dealers to sexually abuse Victoria in exchange for drugs. She declares, "There are many things in my life that I regret, including having you [Vanessa] for a daughter, because that man was your father. But I will not apologize for the decisions I made." Vanessa realizes how much she has allowed her mother's opinions of her to dictate her life, including not allowing herself to love others or be loved. Vanessa responds, "I refuse to let you hold me back anymore. I'm gonna love hard. I'm gonna be a better mother. You don't win because your hand-me-downs stop here." Vanessa continues, "I forgive you with all my might. The scene ends when the two sisters hug and console each other."

Elapsed time: This scene begins at 01:02:55 and ends at 01:09:19 (DVD Scene 12)
Rating: PG-13 for mature thematic material, domestic violence, sex and drug references
Citation: *Madea's Family Reunion* (Lionsgate, 2006) written and directed by Tyler Perry

Maid in Manhattan   INVISIBILITY/OUT-GROUP

Marisa Ventura (Jennifer Lopez) is a single mother born and bred in the boroughs of New York City, who works as a maid in a first-class Manhattan hotel. Through a twist of fate and mistaken identity, Marisa meets Christopher Marshall (Ralph Fiennes), a handsome heir to a political dynasty, who believes that she is a guest at the hotel. Fate steps in and throws the unlikely pair together for one night. When Marisa's true identity is revealed, the two find that they are worlds apart, but the power of love prevails.

Marisa is given the task of going shopping for one of the hotel's rich guests. When she arrives at the counter, the young clerk is on the telephone in what appears to be a personal call. The clerk treats Marisa badly and asks her to step "away" repeatedly. When Marisa attempts to get the clerk to recognize her, the clerk says a snide remark to her friend on the phone about "a maid." Marisa attempts to level the playing field by reminding the clerk, Lisette, about them each being "sisters in the service industry" and that she should service her "low-end customers, because, after all, that is the reason why you're here—unless we're not good enough for you to service." The scene ends after the customers exclaim "You're right."

Elapsed time: This scene begins at 00:14:25 and ends at 00:17:10 (DVD Scene 4)
Rating: PG-13 for some language/sexual references
Citation: *Maid in Manhattan* (Revolution Studios, 2002), written by John Hughes and directed by Wayne Wang

Mona Lisa Smile   DOMINANCE

Miss Katherine Watson (Julia Roberts) is a new member of the art history faculty at the esteemed Wellesley College for women. Set in the 1950s, the women were the smartest in the country and were getting the best education, but were expected to fulfill only the life roles of wife and mother. Miss Watson wanted to challenge all that!

Betty Warren (Kirsten Dunston) is writing an op-ed piece for her school newspaper on the school nurse's decision to provide contraception to the students at Wellesley College. She protests on the stance that she believed that Wellesley "prides itself on propriety." In the editorial she attacks the nurse for being "a cheerleader for promiscuity." Professor Watson (Julia Roberts) is bothered by this article, but another teacher defends Betty's actions saying "Betty's just a young girl flexing her muscles." [Betty's mother is president of the alumni association]. Watson questions if the nurse will get in trouble, and the teacher responds, "Amanda needs to start minding her p's and q's." Later, Amanda has been called into the president's office to defend herself and her twenty one year career at Wellesley. The president informs Amanda that the alumni board has terminated her employment as school nurse.

Elapsed time: This scene begins at 00:22:38 and ends at 00:00:26:47 (DVD Scene 8)
Rating: PG-13 for sexual content and thematic issues
Citation: *Mona Lisa Smile* (Revolution Studios, 2003), written by Lawrence Konner & Mark Rosenthal, directed by Mike Newell

Mona Lisa Smile   GENDER
Miss Katherine Watson (Julia Roberts) is a new member of the art history faculty at the esteemed Wellesley College for women. Set in the 1950s, the women were the smartest in the country and were getting the best education, but were expected to fulfill only the life roles of wife and mother. Miss Watson wanted to challenge all that!

Nancy Abbey (Marcia Gay Harden) is leading the young students in an etiquette class when she presents a scenario. She proposes that a young lady has invited her husband's boss and his wife to their home for dinner to help her husband garner favor as he tries to get a promotion against two rivals. At 6:15 (before a 7:00 dinner), the husband calls and says that the boss has invited the rivals and their spouses as well. She says, "Ever the Wellesley girl, you keep your cool and understand that the boss is probably testing you as much as your husband. What next?" She chides a girl for a flippant answer: "file for divorce." "The thing is," Abbey argues, "it's not a joke. A few years from now, your sole responsibility will be taking care of your husband and children." You may all be here for an easy A, but the grade that matters most is the one he gives you, not me.

Elapsed time: This scene begins at 00:27:54 and ends at 00:00:29:33 (DVD Scene 9)
Rating: PG-13 for sexual content and thematic issues
Citation: *Mona Lisa Smile* (Revolution Studios, 2003), written by Lawrence Konner & Mark Rosenthal, directed by Mike Newell

Mr. Woodcock   POWER/OPPRESSION
Mr. Jasper Woodcock (Billy Bob Thornton) is the meanest gym teacher alive! He calls names, he insults everyone, and he gets violent. He accepts no excuses; in fact, giving excuses is a surefire way to get punished. He is as feared as he is hated, and none more so than by John Farley (Sean William Scott) who learns as an adult that his mom is going to marry Mr. Woodcock. Farley will stop at nothing to keep this from happening.

In the opening scene of this film, Woodcock is excoriating his young protégés. He asks the students a question and then fires a ball into a young boy's gut; and then makes him run laps for not being quick enough to catch the ball. A young man with asthmas is forced to run because he was wheezing. Even a student who correctly answered his question about the capital of Montana was forced to run a lap, citing the only useful tool in life is not knowledge, but "strength of body and strength of mind." While he is lecturing the boys, he suddenly wings a ball at one the boys he had made run laps. A boy named Farley has forgotten his gym clothes and is forced to change out of his street clothes—not in the locker room, but right in the center of the gym floor. Woodcock offers a rental uniform for twenty-five cents, but when Farley tries to explain his situation that someone stole his gym bag, Woodcock cuts him off, preferring to teach Farley "a lesson in personal responsibility." The scene cuts to Farley in his underwear hanging from a pull-up bar. All the while he is attempting to do a chin-up, Woodcock insults the young boy: "You are a disgrace to fat, gelatinous, out-of-shape little kids the world over. I don't tolerate losers in my gymnasium." The scene ends when Woodcock tells Farley "You better not even think of letting go."

Elapsed time: This scene begins at 00:00:20 and ends at 00:04:18 (DVD Scene 1)
Rating: PG-13 for crude and sexual content, thematic material, language, and a mild drug reference
Citation: *Mr. Woodcock* (New Line Cinema, 2007), written by Michael Carnes & Josh Gilbert, directed by Craig Gillespie

Newsies   **CO-OPTATION/POWER**
"And a child shall lead them" could be the slogan for this film about a group of young newsboys who reject their publisher's rate hikes and form a labor union. Pulitzer (Robert Duvall) tries to put the squeeze on the young boys, but jack (Christian Bale) and his cohort refuse to go down without a fight.

Jack Kelly (Christian Bale) has been brought to the office of Joseph Pulitzer, who is talking with him about the appropriateness of war. Pulitzer argues, "People think that wars are about right and wrong. They're not. They're about power." Pulitzer, a journalist, continues, "The power of the press is the greatest power of them all. I tell this city how to think. I tell this city how to vote. I shape its future." He mentions that he is thinking about Jack's own future and says, "I have the power to see that you stay locked in the refuge." Jack interrupts, "And I have the power to break out again." Pulitzer continues, "Or I could see you released tomorrow free and clear with more money in your pockets than you can earn in three lifetimes." Jack challenges Joe for bribing him and Pulitzer shuts him down, saying, "Just shut up and listen to me for once. You work for me until the strike is over. It will end, boy, make no mistake, without you. Then you go wherever you want to buy a ticket for, away from the refuge, these foul streets—free—with money to spend and nobody chasing you." Jack sneers, "I must have you scared pretty bad, old man" but Pulitzer snaps, "I offer you freedom and money just to work for me again. To your friends, I won't be so kind. Now your partner, what's his name, David? I understand he has a family. What do you think the refuge will do to him? And it will be you who put him there, and all the others. After all, you are their leader. Go back to the refuge tonight; think about it. Give me your answer in the morning." The scene ends when Pulitzer pushes Jack out the door.

Elapsed time: This scene begins at 01:24:33 and ends at 01:27:43 (DVD Scene 16)
Rating: PG for fighting and smoking
Citation: *Newsies* (Walt Disney Pictures, 1992) written by Bob Tzudiker & Noni White, directed by Kenny Ortega

The Next Best Thing   **HETEROSEXISM**

On the heels of a failed relationship, Abbie (Madonna) finds solace in the arms of her gay best friend Robert (Rupert Everett); the two spend one chance night of passion together. Abbie gets pregnant and the two attempt to raise the child together while maintaining separate lives.

Abbie and Robert and other friends are attending the funeral of one of their very good friends who has just died from AIDS. They are there to be of comfort to David (Neil Patrick Harris) who is the life partner of the deceased, Joe. The group approaches the interment from the opposite side of the cemetery than the other mourners, and it is obvious that this group is not a welcomed sight. Joe's family members have ignored David's wishes regarding the funeral arrangements. When Abbie asks the identification of the pallbearers, David responds, "A grab bag of Joe's relatives he couldn't relate to. They wouldn't participate in his life, but they'd drive across three states to attend his funeral." Robert asks what Joe is wearing, and David tells how they ignored Joe's request to be buried in jeans and a t-shirt, or at least in his black suit. David reports that the family felt the black suit was "too loud," which they meant "too gay." David contends, "I just wish I could have given him what he wanted. Joe wanted to be cremated; his ashes scattered to the wind in Joshua Tree with Don Mclean's 'American Pie' playing really, really loud on a boom box. The family said 'no.'" David and Joe's mother make eye contact and it is clear that she does not care for David nor his entourage. The priest begins to pray (David objects), and offers consolation to the family for their loss of someone so young, "struck down in his prime by pneumonia." The scene ends as David and friends sing "American Pie."

Elapsed time: This scene begins at 00:12:20 and ends at 00:15:02 (DVD Scene 4)
Rating: PG-13 for mature thematic elements, sexual content, partial nudity and language
Citation: *The Next Best Thing* (Lakeshore Entertainment, 2000), written by Tom Ropelewski, directed by John Schlesinger

The Next Best Thing   **COMPULSORY HETEROSEXUALITY/**
                                                  STEREOTYPE

On the heels of a failed relationship, Abbie (Madonna) finds solace in the arms of her gay best friend Robert (Rupert Everett); the two spend one chance night of passion together. Abbie gets pregnant and the two attempt to raise the child together while maintaining separate lives.

David, Robert, and another friend, Richard, are at Joe's plot at the cemetery and are commiserating over their loss. Robert, who is gay, mentions that he and Abbie (Madonna) had had sex the week before, and that Abbie is now avoiding him. The other two excitedly question him about his tryst, wondering if he is interested in doing it again. Richard asks, "Are you telling us you're straight?" Robert denies this. David and Richard trade barbs, each adding, "Next thing, he'll be combing his hair like Donald Trump;" "And subscribing to *Victoria's Secret* catalogs;" "And voting Republican;" "Praise to Lordy, she's been reformed; call Jerry Falwell." Robert argues, "Don't call me she." Richard responds, "See?"

Elapsed time: This scene begins at 00:25:33 and ends at 00:26:54 (DVD Scene 8)
Rating: PG-13 for mature thematic elements, sexual content, partial nudity and language
Citation: *The Next Best Thing* (Lakeshore Entertainment, 2000), written by Tom Ropelewski, directed by John Schlesinger

The Next Best Thing   COMPULSORY HETEROSEXUALITY/OUT GROUP
On the heels of a failed relationship, Abbie (Madonna) finds solace in the arms of her gay best friend Robert (Rupert Everett); the two spend one chance night of passion together. Abbie gets pregnant and the two attempt to raise the child together while maintaining separate lives.

Robert is at the airport awaiting the arrival of his parents. When they arrive they inquire about Abbie's current love life. Robert admits that Abbie is pregnant with his baby. Robert's father questions, "You mean it was all a joke?...You're not really queer?" Robert admits, "Lower your voice. Of course, I'm queer. I'm just having a baby as well." His father argues, "You're going to make a laughingstock of the family. A child needs someone to look up to." Robert interrupts, "Well, I'll wear heels." Mr. Whittaker threatens, "If you were younger, I'd take you over my knee and thrash the living daylights out of you." The scene ends after Mr. Whittaker storms off to find a taxi.

Elapsed time: This scene begins at 00:31:41 and ends at 00:33:43 (DVD Scene 9)
Rating: PG-13 for mature thematic elements, sexual content, partial nudity and language
Citation: *The Next Best Thing* (Lakeshore Entertainment, 2000), written by Tom Ropelewski, directed by John Schlesinger

North Country   SEXISM
Based on the true story of the first successful sexual harassment suit in America. Josey Aimes (Charlize Theron) and several female employees at a Minnesota mining company face unbearable working conditions including rape, physical and verbal abuse. Josey refuses to endure any longer and vows to bring the company's secret to the public.

Mr. Pearson, owner of Pearson Taconite, is being sued in a class action sexual harassment case and he and his lawyer are discussing his prospects of winning the case. His lawyer, Leslie Conlin (Linda Emond), has suggested that Pearson settle the lawsuit out of court: "If she gets any other women, they'll get their class and you will lose this case." Mr. Pearson questions, "Leslie, why do you think I hired you? Because you're the smartest lawyer I could find? No. I hired you because you were the smartest woman lawyer I could find." He continues, "Do the Minnesota Vikings have to put in a girl quarterback? Of course not. Some things are for men and some things are for women. Mining is men's work." "Like lawyering," Conlin interjects. Pearson follows with, "See, a man would never say something like that. Women take everything too personally." "You're going to take it personally if she wins," Conlin retorts. She begins to explain the possible losses to him financially and to his company's reputation should he lose the case. "A loss here will change the way you run your business. There'll be paid leave for pregnancies. Lawyers to draft sexual harassment policies. Not to mention that you will have helped establish a legal precedent that will affect every single company in America, including the Minnesota Vikings." Pearson comes back: "Except she is not going to win. This woman is a single welfare mother with two kids out of wedlock—a sordid sexual history." The scene ends as Mr. Pearson calls in Bobby Sharp who is set to testify against the woman bringing charges.

Elapsed time: This scene begins at 01:25:41 and ends at 01:27:18 (DVD Scene 19)
Rating: R for sequences involving sexual harassment including violence and dialogue, and for language
Citation: *North Country* (Warner Bros Pictures, 2005), screenplay written by Michael Seitzman, directed by Niki Caro

North Country   SOCIAL JUSTICE
Based on the true story of the first successful sexual harassment suit in America. Josey Aimes (Charlize Theron) and several female employees at a Minnesota mining company face unbearable working conditions including rape, physical and verbal abuse. Josey refuses to endure any longer and vows to bring the company's secret to the public.

Bobby Sharp (Jeremy Renner) has been called to testify regarding his eyewitness account of his former friend, Josey Aimes (Charlize Theron), being raped by a teacher when they were in high school. Prior to this scene, Bobby had been outspoken in his ire towards women working at the mine and is one of the men named in the sexual harassment suit. Sharp denies the rape allegation, painting Josey as a wanton teenager. Josey's lawyer, Bill White (Woody Harrelson), continues to question Sharp with questions (insults) intended to make Sharp angry and possibly get him to tell the truth about his recollection of the event, including how Bobby ran away when he saw the teacher raping Josey. White pushes, "You gonna keep lying about your friend, or are you going to stand up and be a man?" Finally, Sharp breaks and admits the teacher raped Josey, "What was I supposed to do?" White adds, "What are you supposed to do when the ones with all the power are hurting those with none? Well, for starters, you stand up. You stand up and tell the truth. You stand up for your friends. You stand up even when you're all alone. You stand up." The scene ends as other men and women agree to testify about the deplorable working conditions for women at the Pearson mine.

Elapsed time: This scene begins at 01:51:37 and ends at 01:57:58 (DVD Scene 25)
Rating: R for sequences involving sexual harassment including violence and dialogue, and for language
Citation: *North Country* (Warner Bros Pictures, 2005), screenplay written by Michael Seitzman, directed by Niki Caro

Not Another Teen Movie   INVISIBILITY
A new comedy classic taking pot shots at every convention of the teen comedy genre. To win a bet, Jake (Chris Evans) must woo and win the heart of Janey Briggs (Chyler Leigh), a nerdy girl turned hot chick.

Jake (Chris Evans), the star athlete, is having a conversation with his football teammate, Reggie Ray (Ron Lester; reprising his role from *Varsity Blues*), about being cleared to play football after a blood clot the size of a grapefruit was found in Reggie Ray's brain as a result of multiple concussions. Soon, Austin (Eric Christian Olsen) interrupts by taunting Jake's loss of first-string status. Austin opens his locker and hits Reggie Ray in the face. Malik (Deon Richmond), the only African American in the school, stands quietly in the background. Reggie Ray, a bit wobbly and looking like he is going to faint, asks Malik to hold his books for a moment. Malik answers, "Sure, why not? I am the token black guy. I'm just supposed to smile, stay out of the conversation, and say things like 'Damn,' 'Shit,' and 'That is whack!'" The scene ends when Reggie Ray falls to the floor.

Elapsed time: This scene begins at 00:07:35 and ends at 00:08:26 (DVD Scene 2)
Rating: R for strong crude sexual content and humor, language and some drug content
Citation: *Not Another Teen Movie* (Columbia Pictures, 2001), written by Mike Bender & Adam Jay Epstein, directed by Joel Gallen

An Officer and a Gentleman   GENDER/SEXISM
Dissatisfied with his life in a small factory town, John Mayo (Richard Gere) enlists in the armed services. He and his fellow recruits must face down the brim of drill sergeant Foley (Lou Gossett, Jr.) who wants to weed out those soldiers who can't complete the training.

The new recruits are doing physical training and running through the obstacle course. Mayo (Richard Gere) and Worley (David Keith) are the first two to cross the finish line. Sargeant Foley (Louis Gossett, Jr.) is barking orders at the recruits. When Casey Seeger (Lisa Eilbacher), the only female recruit in the squad, has difficulty scaling the climbing wall, Sargeant Foley lashes out at her. He questions, "You really wanna be a man, Seeger? Are you another one of those little girls that didn't get enough of your daddy's attention because he really wanted a son, Seeger?" Seeger begins to cry and Foley chides, "That's what will beat you every time, Seeger—the mental attitude of a person of the female persuasion. Deep down under all that bullshit, you're still thinking like a second class citizen. You can never give orders to men!" He concedes give her permission to walk around the wall but refers to her as "sugar britches."

Elapsed time: This scene begins at 00:25:32 and ends at 00:28:09 (DVD Scene 4)
Rating: R for language, sexuality, and adult themes
Citation: *An Officer and a Gentleman* (Paramount Pictures, 1982), written by Douglas Day Stewart, directed by Taylor Hackford

Parenthood   GENDER

Gil (Steve Martin) is going through a bit of a midlife crisis; he and his wife don't seem to communicate well anymore; he has one son who bangs his head off of walls and another who battles low self esteem. On top of that, he quit his job after being passed over for a promotion.

In a previous scene, Gil (Steve Martin) was passed over for a promotion in his company, and promptly tendered his resignation. In this scene he returns home to find his children and their friends running amuck in the house. He is sharing his story with his wife Karen who tells him that she is pregnant. Gil reacts negatively to this surprise and questions how his wife could have chosen to have gotten pregnant without consulting him; she responds the same (about his decision to quit his job). She encourages him to get his job back, but he argues that if he goes back he'll "be a eunuch." His wife mentions that she was considering going back to work in the fall, and the pregnancy changes her plans. Gil responds, "Well, that's the difference between men and women: women have choices, men have responsibilities." His wife says, "Then I choose for you to have this baby. That's my choice. You have the baby. You get fat. You breastfeed until your nipples are sore. I'll go back to work." Gil laughs, "Let's return from LaLa Land because that ain't gonna happen. Whether I crawl back or get another job, now I'll have less time to spend at home." Karen argues that Gil just wants her to get an abortion and asks him for his honest opinion. Gil responds, "That's a decision every woman has to make on her own." The scene ends as Gil leaves the room.

Elapsed time: This scene begins at 01:26:11 and ends at 01:30:45 (DVD Scene 13)
Rating: PG-13 for some sexuality and some language
Citation: *Parenthood* (Imagine Entertainment, 1989), screenplay written by Lowell Ganz & Babaloo Mandel, directed by Ron Howard

Philadelphia   HOMOPHOBIA/GENDER

Believing he was fired for being gay and having AIDS, attorney Andrew Beckett (Tom Hanks) sues his employers for discrimination and civil rights violations. Taking up his case is ambulance chaser Joe Miller (Denzel Washington) who learns important lessons about tolerance along the way.

Joe (Denzel Washington) has just returned from seeing his doctor, who had suggested that Joe take an AIDS test. Joe and his wife, Lisa, are discussing what Lisa terms Joe's "problem with gays." She questions how many gay people he knows and Joe returns the question; Lisa cites several examples including her Aunt Teresa. Incredulous, Joe questions, "Teresa is gay? That beautiful, sensuous, voluptuous woman is a lesbian? Since when?" Joe adds, "Well, hey, I admit it. I'm prejudiced. I don't like homosexuals. There; you got me." He continues, "I mean the way those guys do that thing [he gestures two fists slamming together]; don't they get confused? [He makes a prancing gesture and high pitched feminine voice] 'I don't know—is that yours or is that mine?' I don't want to be in the bed with anybody that's stronger than me or that has more hair on their chest than I do. Now you can call me old fashioned; you can call me conservative, but just call me a man. Besides, I think you have to be a man to understand how really disgusting that whole idea is anyway." Lisa refers to him as "the caveman of the house," to which Joe responds, "You're damn skippy." Joe turns and walks over to where his baby daughter is sitting in a high chair and tells her, "You stay away from you Aunt Teresa." Lisa chides him, but her angrily returns, "Just think about it; those guys pumping up together trying to be macho and faggot at the same time. I can't stand that shit!" He turns the conversation on Lisa and questions, "I got a question for you. Would you accept a client if you were constantly thinking 'I don't want this person to touch me; I don't even want them to breathe on me?'" Lisa responds, "Not if I were you, honey." Joe agrees.

Elapsed time: This scene begins at 00:33:36 and ends at 00:35:23 (DVD Scene 15)
Rating: PG-13 for graphic language and thematic material
Citation: *Philadelphia* (Tristar Pictures, 1993) written by Ron Nyswaner, directed by Jonathan Demme

Philadelphia   DISCRIMINATION
Believing he was fired for being gay and having AIDS, attorney Andrew Beckett (Tom Hanks) sues his employers for discrimination and civil rights violations. Taking up his case is ambulance chaser Joe Miller (Denzel Washington) who learns important lessons about tolerance along the way.

Joe (Denzel Washington) is reading in the library at the same time as Andrew Beckett (Tom Hanks) is conducting research on employment law. The reference librarian brings Andrew a book and confirms its content related to HIV-related discrimination. The nearby patrons bristle when they hear these words. Soon, the librarian informs Andrew, "We do have a private research room available." Andrew states that he is fine in his current location, but the librarian again offers, questioning "Wouldn't you be more comfortable in the research room?" Andrew returns, "No. Would it make you more comfortable?" Once the librarian leaves, another one of the nearby patrons excuses himself from the table.

Elapsed time: This scene begins at 00:35:46 and ends at 00:38:39 (DVD Scene 16)
Rating: PG-13 for graphic language and thematic material
Citation: *Philadelphia* (Tristar Pictures, 1993) written by Ron Nyswaner, directed by Jonathan Demme

Pocahantas   DISCRIMINATION/DOMINANCE/CO-OPTATION
Return to the founding of the New World when settlers from England found their way into the Virginia waterways. Here, John Smith and his fellow travelers meet

Powhatan and the indigenous people of the land. Conflicts ensue and misunderstandings arise, but amidst all this tension, a new love is born, and it could be the ties that bind these two groups together.

John Smith has just returned to the settlement from scouting the new terrain, where he had met Pocahantas. The governor, Ratcliffe, questions if Smith knows the whereabouts of the local Indians so that he can make a plan of attack to "eliminate these savages once and for all." Smith argues, "We don't have to fight them. They're not savages. They can help us. They know the land; they know how to navigate the rivers." When John shows them the native maize, Ratcliffe interrupts, "They don't want to feed us you ninnies! They want to kill us—all of us! They've got our gold, and they'll do anything to keep it." Ratcliffe refers to the Indians and "murderous thieve" and states "There's no room for their kind in civilzed society." Smith counters, "But this is their land," and Ratcliffe responds, "This is my land! I make the laws here. And I say, anyone who so much as looks at an Indian without killing him on sight will be tried for treason and hanged."

Elapsed time: This scene begins at 00:52:45 and ends at 00:00:54:06 (DVD Scene 19)
Rating: G for general audiences
Citation: *Pocahantas* (Walt Disney Pictures, 1995), written by Carl Binder, directed by Mark Gabriel & Eric Goldberg

The Producers   **STEREOTYPE**
Max Bialystock (Nathan Lane) and his co-worker Leo Bloom (Matthew Broderick) attempt to produce the world's worst musical on Broadway as a means of swindling money from the show's investors.

Max (Nathan Lane) and Mr. Bloom (Matthew Broderick) are visiting the home of renowned theatrical director Roger DeBris. They are greeted at the door by Carmen Ghia, Roger's "common law assistant," who is very effeminate and speaks with an extreme sibilant "s" that is characteristic of gay male stereotypes. Soon Carmen announces Roger's entrance; Roger appears in a sequined gown. Roger notices Bloom's surprise at his wearing a dress and admits he is preparing to attend a masquerade ball and he hopes to win best costume. He chagrins at his costume which is supposed to be of the Grand Duchess Anastasia, but feels it looks more like the Chrysler Building. Max asks Roger to be a part of his drama *Springtime for Hitler*, but Roger declines, citing "The theater's so obsessed with drama so depressed; it's hard to sell a ticket on Broadway. Shows should be more pretty. Shows should be more pretty. Shows should be more...what's the word?" Bloom adds, "Gay?" Roger continues to sing the song, "Keep It Gay." Rogers invites his production team to hear more about the play; he introduces members of his team: one clad in leather, another in a lavender suit, the choreographer wears purple crushed velvet, and the lighting designer is a butch woman. Soon they are joined by a litany of characters reminiscent of the Village People. The scene ends as the entire group forms a conga line and dances off screen.

Elapsed time: This scene begins at 00:44:51 and ends at 00:56:15 (DVD Scene 9)
Rating: PG-13 for sexual humor and references
Citation: *The Producers* (Universal Pictures, 2005), screenplay written by Mel Brooks, directed by Susan Stroman

Racing Stripes — DIFFERENCE/DISCRIMINATION

A young zebra who was rescued after being lost from a circus caravan is being raised by a young girl named Channing Walsh (Hayden Panettiere). Stripes wants to race with the thoroughbreds, but he faces an uphill battle for acceptance.

Stripes the zebra and his owner Channing are attempting to enter Stripes into the local derby races. As they enter the race area, the other jockeys and owners say snide comments about Stripes belonging in a circus or zoo or on a carousel. When the thoroughbred racing horses see Stripes, they begin to make fun of him and call him names. They say, "Haven't you learned? You don't fit in." They call him "freak" and "four left hooves" and tell him to "No freaks allowed. Hoof it! We don't want you!"

Elapsed time: This scene begins at 00:34:01 and ends at 00:34:43 (DVD Scene 11)
Rating: PG for mild crude humor and some language
Citation: *Racing Stripes* (Alcon Entertainment, 2004), screenplay written by David Schmidt, directed by Frederik Du Chau

A Raisin in the Sun — RACISM/DISCRIMINATION

Desiring to leave behind their slum living life, the Younger family purchases a home in an all-White community with insurance funds. The matriarch of the family attempts to help her adult children keep their heads on straight as they come to terms with their new lives. Based on the stage adaptation of Lorraine Hansberry's classic literary text.

The Younger family has just bought a new home in an exclusive all-White community and are packing before the movers arrive. Walter Lee (P. Diddy), his wife Ruth (Audra McDonald), and his sister Beneatha (Sanaa Lathan) are celebrating the upcoming move across town when Mr. Carl Linder (John Stamos) of the Clybourne Park Improvement Association stops by to try to dissuade them from moving. Linder describes the work of the CPIA as a neighborhood watch organization, where they monitor various activities like "block upkeep, special projects" and the New Neighbors Orientation Committee (a welcome wagon of sorts). He shares that the welcome committee has a special category called "Special Community Problems;" the Youngers are one such problem. Mr. Linder mentions his concern about what happens when Blacks move into White neighborhoods. He contends "race prejudice has absolutely nothing to do with this; it's just that the folks in Clybourne Park feel that for the happiness of all concerned, our Negro families are better off—they're happier—living in their own communities." Representing the association "and the collective efforts of our people" Linder offers to buy the house back from the Youngers for a profit. Walter Lee refuses and shows Mr. Linder to the door. Linder responds, "All right, what do you people think you have to gain by moving into a neighborhood where you're not wanted?" He threatens, "You know, people get awful worked up when they feel their whole way of life, everything they ever worked for is threatened. You can't force people to change their hearts, Mr. Younger." The scene ends when Walter Lee closes the door.

Elapsed time: This scene begins at 01:35:45 and ends at 01:40:15 (DVD Scene 21)
Rating: Not Rated
Citation: *A Raisin in the Sun* (Sony Pictures, 2008), screenplay written by Paris Qualles, directed by Kenny Leon

Rush Hour 3   DISCRIMINATION/ETHNOCENTRISM

Detective Carter (Chris Tucker) and Inspector Lee (Jackie Chan) are back for a third installment; this time, they have followed a Chinese criminal kingpin to Paris. The hilarity ensues as Carter and Lee face get caught up with a Chinese gang, the French police, and two very dangerous women.

Upon arrival at the airport in France, Carter and Lee have been stripped and cavity searched by the French police. Hailing a taxi, the driver has a problem with his passengers and demands the two to get out of his cab. Speaking to Lee, the driver turns and says, "I don't drive his kind [speaking of Carter]." Carter speaks up, "My kind?" The driver bluntly answers, "Americans. I don't drive Americans." Lee interrupts, "But I am Chinese." The driver retorts, "Yeah, but you're with him; and they're the most violent people on earth—always starting wars, always killing people. Americans make me sick." He continues, "You're a pathetic bunch of criminals who always resort to violence—always push around the little guy." Carter fires back, "That's not true. America's not violent!" "C'mon, America is a joke. You lost in Vietnam; you lost in Iraq. You can't even beat the Europeans in basketball anymore. The dream team is dead. Even your skinny women disgust me." When the driver challenges the beauty of Halle Berry, Carter pulls out his gun and threatens him. Carter demands the driver to say he loves America and sing the American national anthem.

Elapsed time: This scene begins at 00:28:15 and ends at 00:29:48 (DVD Scene 7)
Rating: PG-13 for sequences of action violence, sexual content, nudity, and language
Citation: *Rush Hour 3* (New Line Cinemas, 2007) written by Jeff Nathanson, directed by Brett Ratner

SLC Punk   DIFFERENCE

Recent college grads Stevo (Matthew Lillard) and Heroin Bob (Michael Goorjian) sport blue Mohawks, listen to hard-core punk and live according to their own rules. Not a problem in many places, but in Salt Lake City they're total outcasts. Add to the mix Stevo's father (Christopher McDonald), who wants his son to study law at Harvard (just as he did). Stevo must decide whether to stay true to his own ideals or start planning for his future.

Stevo, Bob, and Sean have crossed the state line into Wyoming; Stevo narrates "If looking the way we did in Utah was unusual, in the state of Wyoming, affectionately called the Cowboy State, we were fucking aliens." Stevo has blue hair and Bob sports a mohawk, and when the three walk into a local convenience store, they stand out like a sore thumb. The storekeeper asks "What the hell are you?" Stevo sarcastically pretends they are the Magi seeking the Messiah. The storekeeper panics, believing the three have escaped from the state mental institution; Bob calms his down by explaining that they are not crazy, but newly arrived from England: "That's probably why we seem so weird to you, man." The storekeeper's wife enters and questions "What the hell did they do to your hair? My God—you look like a gol-durned Indian." Sean overhears a couple discussing issues of faith. A woman suggests, "That's how come there's so many floods and earthquakes. There is a curse on the land. The end is at hand." Bob argues that floods and earthquakes are nothing new, and the woman responds, 'That is so, but never have so many of Satan's followers been amassed on the earth as there are now." Sean questions, "So you guys have lots of devil worshippers around these parts?" The man responds, "Oh more than ever. They bear the mark." The trio question whether the Nazis were considered devil worshippers, and the local gentleman defends them as "a gathering of people." The woman again mentions the number 666 as the mark of the beast and Stevo pretends to convulse; he moons the couple and shows the tattooed number 666 of his rear end. The store owner chases them from the store with a shotgun; he says, "Told you those boys were trouble."

Elapsed time: This scene begins at 00:43:00 and ends at 00:46:25 (DVD Scene 13)
Rating: R for pervasive language, drug use, violent anti-social behavior and some sexuality
Citation: *SLC Punk* (Beyond Films, 1998), written and directed by James Merendino

Saved!   **DOMINANCE/IN GROUP**
American Eagle High School is the banner school for raising good, wholesome Christian students—the more Christian you are, the more popular. Mary is a good Christian girl with good Christian friends and a good Christian boyfriend. One day, her boyfriend, Dean, informs Mary that he is gay. Crushed, Mary believes that she has been given the task of sacrificing her virginity to save Dean and turn him straight. Once the other students at the school learn of Dean's gayness, Dean is sent to a "de-gayification center" called Mercy House. Mary's got a secret too— she's pregnant—all hell is breaking loose.

Hillary Faye is driving to pick up her friends for school. She first picks up Mary, who has recently made a deal with Jesus to "restore my emotional and spiritual virginity in exchange for curing Dean [of homosexuality]." She has recently received a handicapped accessible van (her vanity license plate reads 'JC [Jesus Christ] GRL') as she drives her wheelchair-bound brother to school. Hillary gives Mary a pin which reads "Christian Jewel" and states, "It's official" that Mary is a member of the in-crowd. Mary asks Roland (Macaulay Calkin) about his summer activities and Roland gives a list of activities that would be nearly impossible for someone who is wheelchair bound. Hillary chastises him, "Why do you have to make people feel so awkward about your differently-abledness?" As she picks up her next friend, Veronica, the narrator describes how Hillary Faye lauds Veronica's adoptive parents' (who had been missionaries in Vietnam) as "an example of God's will triumphing over a savage, godless nation." Hillary applauds herself for giving up a Lexus so that she can drive her brother, Roland, in the accessible van; Veronica agrees that Roland is blessed for having such a caring sister. She mentions how "in some countries like China Hillary Faye would have probably been killed at birth;" Hillary smugly questions, "And then where would you be, Roland?" He answers, "China." Hillary hands Veronica one of the pins and says, "You're one of us now."

Elapsed time: This scene begins at 00:09:04 and ends at 00:11:05 (DVD Scene 4)
Rating: PG-13 for strong thematic issues involving teens — sexual content, pregnancy, smoking and language
Citation: *Saved!* (United Artists, 2004), written and directed by Brian Dannelly

Saving Silverman   **COMPULSORY HETEROSEXUALITY**
Trouble and laughs come in spades when clueless losers Wayne (Steve Zahn) and J.D. (Jack Black) conspire to prevent their best buddy, hapless sad-sack Darren (Jason Biggs), from marrying shrewish Judith (Amanda Peet). Wayne and J.D. will stop at nothing to "save" their friend, including setting him up with long-lost love – and soon-to-be nun – Sandy (Amanda Detmer).

Wayne (Steve Zahn) and J.D. (Jack Black) have kidnapped Judith (Amanda Peet) and are holding her prisoner in the basement of their house. In this scene, Wayne is readjusting Judith's restraints after she had gotten free after convincing J.D. to let her go. When Wayne comes back upstairs, J.D. states that Judith helped him realize that he is gay. Wayne states, "I see what happened. She messed with your head." J.D. emphatically argues, "Wayne, I'm gay," to which Wayne remarks, "No you're not. You're just unsuccessful with women." "No, I'm gay," J.D. responds, "Judith got me in touch with the inner J.D." "How did she do that," Wayne asks. "She listened. Unlike people who have known me for years and ignored all the telltale signs, like my obsession with Bette Midler, my preference for track lighting; oh, and the fact that I like sucking..." "What," Wayne interrupts, "you've done that?" "No, but remember when I bought that book on yoga?" "That's it! I don't want to hear anymore!" Wayne argues, "Look, you want to be gay, that's fine! No problem. But from now on, I'll take care of Judith myself." J.D. questions, "You want to be gay with me?" Wayne screams, "No" and rushes out of the room to end the scene.

Elapsed time: This scene begins at 00:55:05 and ends at 00:56:20 (DVD Scene 18)
Rating: PG-13 for crude and sexual humor, language, and thematic material
Citation: *Saving Silverman* (Columbia Pictures, 2001), written by Hank Nelken & Greg DePaul, directed by Dennis Dugan

School Ties   ANTI-SEMITISM

In the elite world of private preparatory schools, coming from the right stock is essential; those born on the wrong side of the tracks often are excluded. Dabid Greene (Brendan Fraser), a working class teen on scholarship to an exclusive school is widely accepted because of his football prowess, but he faces numerous struggles once the students find out his Jewish heritage.

Dylan (Matt Damon) has just entered the locker room where the rest of the team is showering [warning; there is partial male nudity in this clip]. He enters the shower and David (Fraser) congratulates him on a well-played game. Dylan begins to tell how the "old boys club" bought them the victory; when questioned about his comment, he begins to tell a joke: "True story—last weekend there was a religious revival at Madison Square Garden. Bishop Fulton Sheen gave such a stirring address that afterwards, ten thousand people converted to Catholicism. Then Billy Graham got up and after an hour of inspired preaching ten thousand people converted to Protestantism. Finally, to end the program, Pat Boone got up and sang 'There's a Gold Mine in the Sky,' and twenty thousand Jews joined the Air Force." The other students erupted in laughter, except David, who was seething. Dylan looked at him and asked, "What's the matter David; don't the Jews have a sense of humor?" Dylan turns to his stunned friends, "It turns out our golden boy here is a lying, backstabbing kike." The two fight.

Elapsed time: This scene begins at 01:10:33 and ends at01:12:20 (DVD Scene 12)
Rating: PG-13 for language
Citation: *School Ties* (Paramount Pictures, 1992) screenplay written by Dick Wolf & Darryl Ponicsan, directed by Robert Mandel

School Ties   DIFFERENCE

In the elite world of private preparatory schools, coming from the right stock is essential; those born on the wrong side of the tracks often are excluded. Dabid Greene (Brendan Fraser), a working class teen on scholarship to an exclusive school is widely accepted because of his football prowess, but he faces numerous struggles once the students find out his Jewish heritage.

David enters his room and his roommate, Chris (Chris O'Donnell), is avoiding his gaze. After he removes a Star of David necklace from a drawer where he had kept it hidden, David asks Chris, "Are you going to keep your face hidden in that book for the rest of the year?" Chris wonders, "What do you expect me to say?" David responds, "That it's no big deal." "If it's no big deal, then why did you just tell me in the first place? I'm your roommate." David adds, "You never told me what religion you are." Chris mentions that he is Methodist and David scoffs that he was unaware of that fact. Chris argues that "Jews are different. It's not like the difference between Methodists and Lutherans; I mean, Jews, everything about them is different."

Elapsed time: This scene begins at 01:12:25 and ends at 01:13:41 (DVD Scene 12)
Rating: PG-13 for language

Citation: *School Ties* (Paramount Pictures, 1992) screenplay written by Dick Wolf & Darryl Ponicsan, directed by Robert Mandel

September Dawn   DIFFERENCE

Based on a true story of an 1857 massacre, 120 men and women were slaughtered by Mormon militiamen and Paiute Indians as they made their way across the Utah mountains.

Jacob, the son of the Mormon bishop, had been sent to infiltrate the "Gentile" immigrant camp to spy on their activities. What he was not prepared for was to fall in love with the pastor's daughter. The two are walking up a hillside discussing their family backgrounds when Jacobs mentions that he has never been around Gentiles before. She questions his use of the term since Jacob is Mormon, not Jewish. Jacob responds, "It's just we call you people." She bristles at this term and he defends himself by saying that it is just a different way of speaking—"You know, different parts of the country have different ways of saying things." Jacob mentions how "different" the young girl is from other girls he knows—above anything else, she speaks her mind. She argues that all the women in her clan are outspoken, especially Nancy (Jacob refers to her as "the woman who wears the pants and carries a gun" unlike the other women). Jacob admits that his father thinks Nancy is "an abomination." She argues that in a free country Nancy should be able to dress any way she pleases. Jacob defends his father's rights as bishop to judge others and determine the rules—"to keep people in line" and to therefore determine what is right and normal.

Elapsed time: This scene begins at 00:34:18 and ends at 00:38:00 (DVD Scene 13)
Rating: R for violence
Citation: *September Dawn* (Black Diamond Pictures, 2007), screenplay written by Carole Whang Schutter and Christopher Cain, directed by Christopher Cain

September Dawn   CO-OPTATION

Based on a true story of an 1857 massacre, 120 men and women were slaughtered by Mormon militiamen and Paiute Indians as they made their way across the Utah mountains.

In a previous scene, the bishop (Jon Voigt) had announced his plans to attack the Gentiles because they had been "cursed by God." Here, he and his fellow minister go to the chieftains of the Pauite Indian nation to ask for their assistance in carrying out the plans. The bishop believes that the Gentiles have plans to attack and through his minister (acting as translator) tells the Indians that the Gentiles will also attack them [none of this is accurate]. The translator tells the chiefs that the wagon train has poisoned the water and corn of a nearby nation—"These Gentiles mean to rob and butcher everyone in their way." He tells them "we must stick together" in order to vanquish their foes. The minister tells the chief that the "honor [of killing the immigrants] is to you and your braves. The booty is your reward." The chief rejects this offer questioning why only the Indians must do the killing and face death. He promises the chief that the braves will be protected and will not die. He promises "in return we will help the Paiutes against all your enemies. We will always be with the Paiutes' side in case of war." He closes with the thought "Aren't we all Mormons?" The chiefs agree to participate in the war against the emigrants.

Elapsed time: This scene begins at 01:07:12 and ends at 01:08:55 (DVD Scene 22)
Rating: R for violence
Citation: *September Dawn* (Black Diamond Pictures, 2007), screenplay written by Carole Whang Schutter and Christopher Cain directed by Christopher Cain

She's the Man   SEXISM
Viola (Amanda Bynes) is a star soccer player who learns that the girls' soccer team is being eliminated by budget cuts. Unable to join the boys' soccer team as a girl, she decided to pretend to be her twin brother, Sebastian and earned a spot on the team. Who would have imagined the trouble that she would find herself/himself in as she/he falls in love with her roommate and teammate—he just happens to think that she is a guy.

Viola (Amanda Bynes) is playing soccer on the beach with her boyfriend, Justin, and other teenagers. Nick tells her that she plays better than half of the boys on his team. Later, Viola and her teammates learn that the school has cut the girls' soccer team for lack of participation. The girls appeal to the boys' soccer coach who offers his support—"If there's anything I can do, just say the word." Viola requests to make the soccer team co-ed; the coach responds, "Anything besides that." Soon, Justin and his teammates gather around. The coach offers "You are all excellent players, but girls aren't as fast as boys. Or as strong. Or as athletic. This is not men talking; it's scientific fact. Girls can't beat boys. It's as simple as that." Viola turns to him to support her cause, but he scoffs at the idea. When Viola reminds him of his comments about her skill, Justin attempts to save face in front of his friends by assuming an assertive tone and posture and states, "Viola, end of discussion!" The scene ends when Viola and the girls walk away.

Elapsed time: This scene begins at 00:01:00 and ends at 00:05:50 (DVD Scene 1)
Rating: PG-13 for some sexual material
Citation: *She's the Man* (Dreamworks Pictures, 2006), written by Ewan Leslie, Karen Lutz, & Kirsten Smith, directed by Andy Fickman

South Park: Bigger, Longer, and Uncut   RACISM/DISCRIMINATION
Believing their sons have been unduly influenced after watching an inappropriate film, parents convince the American government to wage war against Canada, Satan, and Saddam Hussein.

The American military is gearing up for a much anticipated war with Canada. The general is giving marching orders to the assembled troops. The general mentions that he has learned that the Canadians are aware of the invasion, so he wants the teams to strategize their attack plan. He announces "Each team has a specific code name and mission." He asks Battalion 5 to raise their hands; the entire squad is African American. He tells them, "You will be the all important first wave attack which we will call Operation Human Shield." Chef (voiced by Isaac Hayes) is a member of Battalion 5, interrupts, but the general keeps going. "Keep in mind, Operation Human Shield will suffer heavy losses." He then addresses Battalion 14 (standing next to Battalion 5). "You are Operation Get Behind the Darkies. You will follow Battalion Five here, and try not to get killed." A hologram shows the teams in battle and the black squad is getting gunned down one by one. The general asks for questions; Chef asks, "Have you ever heard of the Emancipation Proclamation?" The general responds, "I don't listen to hip hop."

Elapsed time: This scene begins at 00:47:45 and ends at 00:48:36 (DVD Scene 17)
Rating: R for pervasive vulgar language and crude sexual humor, and for some violent images
Citation: *South Park: Bigger, Longer, and Uncut* (Comedy Central Films, 1999), written by Trey Parker & Matt Stone, directed by Trey Parker

The Stepford Wives   GENDER/SEXISM
Flashback to "happier" times when women served their men, cooked and cleaned for them, and was their happiest when they got the newest kitchen appliance. But wait, this isn't 1950s; it's the 21ˢᵗ century. Joanna Eberhart (Nicole Kidman) is a former TV exec who has lost her job and her family has moved to Stepford, Connecticut. To her surprise and dismay, this little sleepy town is a throwback to a bygone era.

The men of Stepford are enjoying some time at the local men's association playing war with remote control tanks. The object of the game is to remove the bra from what appears to be a "female" tank. Mike Wellington (Christopher Walken) comments that "only one can survive" and the men begin cheering for Zeus, the "male" tank. At the end of the match, one man screams, "Zeus rules the universe;" while another cheers, "Ahh, to be a man!" Walter (Matthew Broderick), the winner of the match, was to receive $20.00 from Ted. The guys settle down to discuss how Walter is faring in his new town; Walter admits "It's like the way life was meant to be." Meanwhile, Joanna (Walter's wife) is attending the Stepford Book Club where the women discuss great works of literature. Joanna attempts to discuss a book about the life of Lyndon Johnson, when Claire Wellington (Glenn Close) stops her to discuss "probably the most important book any of us will ever read...*Christmas Keepsakes and Collectibles*" (for home decorating). The women cheer and begin to revel about the numerous crafts they can make with pinecones. The scene returns to the men's club where the men are comparing their wives to Joanna—suggesting that she needs to change and become like the other wives. To prove how much better the Stepford wives are, Ted commands his wife to come into the room. He wants to pay Walter the money he owes him; Ted tells his wife that he needs the money. The wife inserts the debit card into her mouth and money ejects from her mouth like an ATM machine and then Ted presses a button on a remote control and turns her "off." Later, Joanna (like a dutiful Stepford wife) has made a roomful of cupcakes for her family so that they can be "proud" of her. Walter's friend , Dave (Jon Lovitz) and his wife, Bobbie (Bette Midler) open the door and Dave asks for the "*man* of the house." Joanna offers them cupcakes and Dave chastises his wife for not baking, and she in turn questions why he doesn't do the baking. He responds, "Because I have a penis." The two men exit the house heading towards the lodge, and Joanna asks Walter when he plans to be home. Walter defiantly responds, "When I'm home" and the two drive away.

Elapsed time: This scene begins at 00:037:19 and ends at 00:45:35 (DVD Scene 8)
Rating: PG-13 for sexual content, thematic material and language
Citation: *The Stepford Wives* (Paramount Pictures, 2004), written by Paul Rudnick, directed by Frank Oz

Sweeney Todd   **DISCRIMINATION/INVISIBILITY**
Johnny Depp (in an Oscar-nominated role) reteams with director Tim Burton for this adaptation of the hit Broadway musical about the Demon Barber of Fleet Street. Depp plays Sweeney Todd, a man who becomes a deranged murderer seeking revenge after being falsely imprisoned. To add to the macabre nature of his crimes, he enlists the help of his lover, Mrs. Lovett (Helena Bonham Carter), who disposes of the victims by baking them into meat pies – sought after by all of London.

A young boy named Toby is harking outside Mrs. Lovett's restaurant where they are unveiling the new and improved meat pies (made of the victims of Todd's butchery). Toby sings his invitations while Mrs. Lovett is serving the well dressed patrons; Mrs. Lovett also directs Toby to serve the various guests. The activity is being watched from across the street by a haggard-looking old woman. As the woman approaches, Mrs. Lovett orders Toby to "throw the old woman out." The scene ends when Toby closes the door in the old woman's face.

Elapsed time: This scene begins at 01:19:03 and ends at 01:21:40 (DVD Scene 18)
Rating: R for graphic, bloody violence
Citation: *Sweeney Todd: The Demon Barber of Fleet Street* (Dreamworks Pictures & Warner Bros. Pictures, 2007), screenplay written by John Logan, directed by Tim Burton

Swing Vote   **COMPULSORY HETEROSEXUALITY/CO-OPTATION**
It's Election Day, and the eyes of the nation have fallen on one beer-swigging couch potato named Bud Johnson (Kevin Costner), who, through no fault of his own, finds himself in the position of being able to single-handedly choose the next American president.

Bud (Kevin Costner) is being interviewed by Kate Madison (Paula Patton), a local reporter, on his stances on particular importance in the presidential election. Her first question is centered on gay marriage. Bud complains, "Ah, shit! Do we, uh, do we have to?" Kate assumes, "So you're against it?" Bud answers, "No, I did not say that." Madison continues, "Then what is your position," to which Bud indicates, "Well, I don't have a position, alright. To tell you the truth, I don't give a rat's ass about it. My dad always said, 'Whatever a king does in his own castle is his business.' OK? I guess the same can go for two, uh, I guess the same can go for two queens." Since Bud's vote is the only one that counts, each of the candidates are tailoring their positions to fit Bud's ideals. A political ad appears with the president of the United States (Kelsey Grammer) advocating for gay marriage. In the ad, the president wants to introduce "a few friends of mine." He declares, "They're our doctors and our peace officers. They teach our children, they serve nobly in our armed forces. For too long, homosexual Americans have been persecuted by the country they love. That's why this president, if re-elected, will implement the Open Door Initiative. Gay Americans, men and women alike, will be able to proudly step out of the closet and on to the altar, to exchange the sacred vows enjoyed by the rest of us. Bud, with your help, this Republican administration, will say 'I do' to gay marriage." The people standing with the president state "I do." Most of them project stereotypical images: men with lisps, deep voiced women with masculine uniforms, etc. The scene concludes with the president and his friends in the shape of a triangle standing atop a rainbow flag.

Elapsed time: This scene begins at 01:14:49 and ends at 01:17:41 (DVD Scene 9)
Rating: PG-13 for language
Citation: *Swing Vote* (Touchstone Pictures, 2008) written by Jason Richman & Joshua Michael Stern, directed by Joshua Michael Stern

Swing Vote   **DOMINANCE/PREJUDICE**
It's Election Day, and the eyes of the nation have fallen on one beer-swigging couch potato named Bud Johnson (Kevin Costner), who, through no fault of his own, finds himself in the position of being able to single-handedly choose the next American president.

Bud (Kevin Costner) is working on the assembly line of an egg factory. He and two of his coworkers are discussing the recent layoffs of some of the other employees. In discussing Dewey, Walter (Judge Reinhold) reports, "Bullshit! He got insourced. Instead of exporting our jobs to Mexico, they're importing Mexicans to take our jobs." Bud calls Walter paranoid; just then, a person speaking in Spanish blares over the loudspeaker. Walter continues, "I can't even read the damn signs no more. Our days are numbered, fellas; you mark my words. These hombres work twice as hard for half the money." Bud defends, "yeah, well, I just figure they need this job twice as bad as us." Walter questions, "Well, who's side are you on?" Bud adds, "Well, I don't take sides, Lowell; just stating the obvious." Walter complains, "Next thing you know, they'll be taking away our right to vote." The scene closes with Bud stating that voting is a social contract, while admitting that he does not know who he is voting for.

Elapsed time: This scene begins at 00:06:54 and ends at 00:08:13 (DVD Scene 1)
Rating: PG-13 for language

Citation: *Swing Vote* (Touchstone Pictures, 2008) written by Jason Richman & Joshua Michael Stern, directed by Joshua Michael Stern

Tears of the Sun   **SOCIAL JUSTICE**

Bruce Willis stars as Lt. A.K. Waters, a heroic Navy S.E.A.L. who defies military orders and follows his conscience in director Antoine Fuqua's epic action drama. Sent to the jungles of embattled Africa to rescue a doctor (Monica Bellucci), Waters realizes he must also save the refugees in her care – even if it endangers him and his troops and places his military career in jeopardy.

Lt. Waters (Bruce Willis) and his team are attempting to rescue dozens of African refugees from certain death by a genocidal militia. They are hoping to get to the American outpost in Cameroon, but the path is risky and they are sorely outnumbered by the enemy. Some of the soldiers and refugees have already been killed, and the rest are in grave danger. Lt. Waters explains that his risks in the mission have placed them all in harm's way, and getting them to safety is going to be tough. His commanding officer tells him to abandon the refugees and only rescue the Americans, but Waters cannot leave the people in danger. He gives the soldiers an opportunity to speak freely about their feelings on leaving the refugees or continuing on with them. The first soldier to speak argues, "In my opinion, sir, we cut our losses. This isn't our fucking war." Another chimes in, "Let's get these people to safety." Still another adds, "I can't leave them, sir." Red, a soldier who was initially against the mission, admits, "I can't look at them like packages [code word initially given at the outset of the mission] anymore. I'm gonna get them out or I'm gonna die trying." Zee, the only African American soldier, adds his final comments, "L.T., those Africans are my people too. For all the years that we were told to stand down and to stand by…you're doing the right thing." The two bump fists and Waters says to Zee, "For our sins." The scene ends when the team climbs the hill.

Elapsed time: This scene begins at 01:24:23 and ends at 01:27:35 (DVD Scene 21)
Rating: R for strong war violence, some brutality and language
Citation: *Tears of the Sun* (Cheyenne Enterprises, 2003) written by Alex Lasker & Patrick Cirillo, directed by Antoine Fuqua

To Kill a Mockingbird   **RACISM/PREJUDICE**
Set in a small Alabama town during the Depression, this adaptation of Harper Lee's Pulitzer Prize-winning novel follows Atticus Finch (Gregory Peck), a lawyer who defends an innocent black man (Brock Peters) against rape charges, but winds up in a fury of hate and prejudice. Finch's children, Jem and Scout (Phillip Alford and Mary Badham), soon learn lessons about race, class, justice and the pain of growing up.

Atticus Finch (Gregory Peck) is a lawyer and is in court defending the life of Tom Robinson, a black man accused of raping a white woman. During his summation, Finch refutes the testimony of the plaintiff and the witnesses, citing their prejudice as the root of their allegations. He argues that the plaintiff accused Robinson out of her own guilt, for she had broken a "rigid and time honored code of our society" for kissing a black man. "She did something that in our society is unspeakable." Finch speaks of the plaintiff's and the witnesses' testimonies "evil assumption that all Negroes lie, all negroes are basically immoral beings, all Negro men are not to be trusted around our women." The scene ends when Finch proclaims, "In the name of God, I believe Tom Robinson."

Elapsed time: This scene begins at 01:31:39 and ends at 01:38:40 (DVD Scene 28)
Rating: NR
Citation: *To Kill a Mockingbird* (Brentwood Productions, 1962), screenplay written by Horton Foote, directed by Robert Mulligan

Twelve Angry Men   PREJUDICE/STEREOTYPE

A guilty verdict means death – but the jury's not about to let that spoil their day. Twelve men must decide the fate of an 18-year-old boy accused of fatally stabbing his father. Only one (Henry Fonda) wants to take the time to coolly deliberate the case.

The jury is casting ballots to convict or acquit a young teenager; the vote comes to 9-3 in favor of acquittal. One juror who voted against the defendant goes on a tirade saying: "I don't understand you people. I mean, all these picky little points you keep bringing up; they don't mean anything. You saw this kid just like I did. You're not going to tell me you believe that phony story about losing the knife and being at the movies. Look, you know how these people lie; it's born in them. I mean, what the heck, I don't have to tell you. They don't know what the truth is; and let me tell you, they don't need any real big reason to kill someone either, no sir." One of the frustrated jurors stands and walks away from the table, but the man continues. "They get drunk; they're real big drinkers, all of them, you know that; and then bang, someone's lying in the gutter. Nobody's blaming them for it; it's just the way they are by nature. You know what I mean, violent? Human life don't mean as much to them as it does to us." Others continue to stand and turn their backs on the speaker, but he continues to make his case: "Look, they're lushing it up and fighting all the time; and, if somebody gets killed, then somebody gets killed. They don't care. Sure, they're some good things about them, too; look, I'm the first one to say that I've known a couple who are OK but that's the exception, you know what I mean? Most of the time, it's like they have no feeling; they can do anything." As more and more men walk away from the table and begin to turn their backs on him, he turns and says, "What's going on here? I'm trying to tell you; you're making a big mistake, you people. This kid is a liar; I know it. I know all about them. Listen to me; they're no good. There's not a one of them any good." The scene ends when the speaker sits down by himself.

Elapsed time: This scene begins at 01:17:35 and ends at 01:20:00 (DVD Scene 13)
Rating: NR
Citation: *Twelve Angry Men* (Metro Goldwyn Meyer, 1957), written by Reginald Rose, directed by Sidney Lumet

Underworld   **ETHNOCENTRISM/DISCRIMINATION**

Vampires and werewolves have waged a nocturnal war against each other for centuries. But all bets are off when a female vampire warrior named Selene (Kate Beckinsale), who's famous for her strength and werewolf-hunting prowess, becomes smitten with a peace-loving male werewolf, Michael (Scott Speedman), who wants to end the war.

The scene opens with a gruesome scene of Lucian, a member of the Lycan (werewolf) race being whipped bloody; he is chained to the floor and is required to watch his bride, Sonja, a vampire, be chained to a post as the sun rises above her. She is burned alive. Victor, Sonja's father, oversees these grim proceedings. When she is killed, Lucian changes from human to vampire and breaks free from his chains and throws Victor out of the room. The scene breaks to present day when Michael Covinus is awakened from the 600-year flashback. Michael is a pureblood vampire and Lucian has taken some of his blood to add to his own to recreate himself as a powerful hybrid. Michael tells Lucian that he saw what happened; he says, "that's what started the war [between the vampires and Lycans]." Lucian tells Michael, "We were slaves once—the daylight guardians of the vampires. I was born in servitude, yet I harbored them no ill will—even took a vampire for my bride. It was forbidden our union. Victor feared a blending of the species. He feared it so much he killed her—his own daughter burned alive—for loving me. This is his war—Victor's. He spent the last 600 years exterminating my species." The scene ends when two armed men walk in the room.

Elapsed time: This scene begins at 01:23:27 and ends at 01:28:58 (DVD Scene 20)
Rating: R for graphic, bloody violence
Citation: *Underworld* (Lakeshore Entertainment, 2003), written by Kevin Grevioux & Len Wiseman, directed by Len Wiseman

Varsity Blues   **POWER/OUT-GROUP**

In a small town in Texas, there is one phenomenon that binds the entire town together—high school football. The only route to success is on the gridiron, and fate brings popularity for one second string quarterback, Jonathan "Mox" Moxon (James Van Der Beek), when the star quarterback is injured. Add a psycho-serious coach with a win-at-all-costs philosophy, and the stage is set for a mutiny on the football field.

Mox (James Vanderbeek) is the quarterback of his high school football team and after practice, Coach Kilmer (John Voigt) asks him to stay to talk. Kilmer is giving Mox instructions on how to defeat their opponents in the next game. Mox seems disinterested. Kilmer questions, "Are you hearing me? You disobey me and I'll bury you. I know about your scholarship to Brown [University]; I got your grades under review, and don't you think for a minute that I can't fuck with your transcripts and get this whole deal blown for you. I get what I want, and you get what you want—that's it." Later that evening, Mox goes to talk with his ex-girlfriend,

Jules (Amy Smart), about his college acceptance. He also explains that "Kilmer is threatening to fuck up my scholarship if I don't play by his rules tomorrow." She tells him to quit because it is just a football game, but he states that he can't because "if it was just football, I'd play. I love football when it's pure. If I play for Kilmer tomorrow, and we win; he wins. Everyone in West Cain will go on believing he's the best coach that ever lived. What about the next team he coaches? And the one after that? What if my little brother ends up playing for him? I would be buying into everything that's wrong with this town." Jules quips, "You want some cheese with that whine? Why don't you just step up and play the hero? C'mon Mox, you're a football guy, you mean you don't know about heroes?" Mox returns, "Yeah, but heroes win. What if I lose?"

Elapsed time: This scene begins at 01:15:45 and ends at 01:18:47 (DVD Scene 17)
Rating: R for strong language throughout, sexuality and nudity, and some substance abuse
Citation: *Varsity Blues* (Tova Laiter Production, 1999), written by Peter Iliff, directed by Brian Robbins

Walk the Line   **DOMINANCE**
Based on the life of the iconic Johnny Cash (Joaquin Phoenix), this film follows Cash's transformation from man to icon – from his hardscrabble days on an Arkansas farm to Sun Records in Memphis, Tenn., where Cash finally found a way for his talent to come into its own as a country music star.

June Carter (Reese Witherspoon) is shopping in the local general store when she is stopped by several of her fans who enjoy her music and are looking forward to seeing her concert later that evening. As she continues shopping, the store clerk mentions to June, "You know, your ma and pa are good Christians in a world gone to pot. I'm surprised they still speak to you after that stunt with Carl Smith. Divorce is an abomination. Marriage is for life." The scene ends as June admits, "I'm sorry I let you down, ma'am" and walks away.

Elapsed time: This scene begins at 00:54:08and ends at 00:55:40 (DVD Scene 16)
Rating: PG-13 for some language, thematic material and depiction of drug dependency
Citation: *Walk the Line* (Fox 2000 Pictures, 2006) written by Gill Dennis and James Mangold, directed by James Mangold

Welcome to the Dollhouse   **OPPRESSION**
A tragic tale of 11-year-old Dawn Weiner and her experiences as an unpopular pre-teen in junior high school. Dawn is teased by her classmates, faces the daily threat by the school bully, and has a secret crush on her older brother's friend.

Dawn (Heather Matarazzo) enters the cafeteria and is searching for a place to sit; most of the students either ignore her or refuse to allow her to sit down at their table. She finds a person who is sitting alone and asks to sit down. Soon after, a group of cheerleaders approach the table and ask Dawn if she is a lesbian. They begin chanting "Lesbo, Lesbo, Lesbo" as they walk away.

Elapsed time: This scene begins at 00:01:50 and ends at 00:04:00 (DVD Scene 1)
Rating: R for language
Citation: *Welcome to the Dollhouse* (Suburban Pictures, 1995), written and directed by Todd Solondz

We Were Soldiers   **PRIVILEGE**
In the first major battle of the Vietnam War, 450 gung-ho Army dogfaces square off for one month against 2,000 North Vietnamese regulars in the Ia Drang Valley. Mel Gibson's a lieutenant colonel who exhorts his men to be all they can be, and Barry Pepper plays a reporter who draws a bead on the story.

The wives and girlfriends of the active soldiers have gathered to introduce new members to the community. They discuss various places to get certain services like groceries and the like. When the subject of the better Laundromats comes up, one wife questions the efficacy of a laundry that disallows colored clothes from being laundered there because the sign in the window indicates "Whites only." The room falls silent and the other women begin looking at Alma Givens (Simbi Khali), the only African American in the room. Alma politely scolds the young woman, "They mean white people only." The young woman responds, "That's awful. Your husband is wearing the uniform of a country that allows a place to say his laundry's not good enough, when he could die for—I'm sorry." Alma responds, "That's alright, honey. I know what my husband's fighting for, and that's why I can smile. My husband will never ask for respect, and he'll give respect to no man who hasn't earned it. Anybody who doesn't respect that can keep his washing machine 'cause my baby's clothes are going to be clean anyway." The ladies chuckle as the scene closes upon a young woman going into labor.

Elapsed time: This scene begins at 00:19:24 and ends at 00:21:25 (DVD Scene 4)
Rating: R for sustained sequences of graphic war violence, and for language
Citation: *We Were Soldiers* (Icon Entertainment International, 2002), written by Harold Moore & Joseph Galloway, directed by Mel Gibson

We Were Soldiers   **SOCIAL JUSTICE**
In the first major battle of the Vietnam War, 450 gung-ho Army dogfaces square off for one month against 2,000 North Vietnamese regulars in the Ia Drang Valley. Mel Gibson's a lieutenant colonel who exhorts his men to be all they can be, and Barry Pepper plays a reporter who draws a bead on the story.

The battalion has been called up to go to combat in the Vietnam War. Lt. Colonel Hal Moore (Mel Gibson) is giving the corps their marching orders, a pep talk of sorts. "Look around you," he says, "in the 7th Cavalry, we got a captain from the Ukraine, another from Puerto Rico. We've got Japanese, Chinese, Blacks, Hispanics, Cherokee Indians. Jews and Gentiles. All Americans." He continues, "Now, here in the States, some men in this unit may experience discrimination because of race or creed; but for you and me now, all that is gone. We're moving into the valley of the shadow of death where you will watch the back of the man next to you as he will watch yours. And you won't care what color he is or by what name he calls God." Moore mentions that he is not going to promise an easy mission, nor will he guarantee that all of them would return alive. He says, "We are going into battle with against a tough and determined enemy" and promises that he will be an active participant in the battle ahead. He maintains, "I will leave no man behind. Dead or alive, we will all come home together. So help me God."

Elapsed time: This scene begins at 00:32:39 and ends at 00:35:05 (DVD Scene 6)
Rating: R for sustained sequences of graphic war violence, and for language
Citation: *We Were Soldiers* (Icon Entertainment International, 2002), written by Harold Moore & Joseph Galloway, directed by Mel Gibson

Who's Your Caddy?   **DISCRIMINATION/RACISM**
Atlanta rap mogul C-Note (OutKast's Big Boi) shakes up the local establishment when he tries to join a stuffy golf club. Despite the objections of the blowhard board president (Jeffrey Jones), C-Note and his entourage stop at nothing to get "in da club." But when C-Note learns that his family legacy is at stake, he finds a bigger reason to end the club's unfair system.

Christopher Hawkins "aka C-Note" (OutKast's Antwan 'Big Boi' Patton) is a successful hip hop recording artist. He and his entourage and publicist (Sherri Shepherd; *The View*) desire to make application to the very exclusive Carolina Hills Country Club. The scene begins with a serene view of life at the country club overdubbed by a classical music soundtrack. This placid community is juxtaposed against C-Note's loud rap music playing as he approaches the club. As the group enters the country club, the members (all White males) are astonished by the prospective members. Meanwhile, in the board room, Mr. Cummings, the president of the club and others are reviewing potential candidates including former President Bill Clinton, Rosie O'Donnell, and the Rev. Al Sharpton, all of whose applications were denied. When referring to Rosie, the president chides "dykes on spikes" as another member calls her a man. When Sharpton's picture comes on the screen, the president winces and denies the application immediately. C-Note and the others are brought into the board room and are treated poorly. When C-Notes requests an application for membership, the president tells his assistant to take them to the Caddy Master as the club is "always looking for an enterprising young man who can carry a bag." The group of African American rap stars are bristled by this suggestion, to wit, Mr. Cummings offers a job in the stables instead. C-Note offers to pay double the membership fee; Mr. Cummings describes the lengthy wait list of over six hundred "very qualified candidates" and mentions that although the club only has 180 members, "there is not a chance in hell that you will be number 181." The scene ends as C-Note places an offer to purchase a palatial home on the 17th hole of the golf course.

Elapsed time: This scene begins at 00:00:31and ends at 00:08:20 (DVD Scene 1)
Rating: PG-13 for crude and sexual content, some nudity, and drug material
Citation: *Who's Your Caddy?* (Our Stories Films and Dimensions Films, 2007), written by Don Michael Paul, Bradley Allenstein, & Robert Henny; directed by Don Michael Paul

Windtalkers   PREJUDICE

Joe Enders (Nicolas Cage) is a gung-ho Marine assigned to protect a "windtalker" – one of several Navajo Indians who were used to relay messages during World War II because their spoken language was indecipherable to Japanese code breakers. Part of Cage's mission, however, is to kill windtalker Ben Yahzee (Adam Beach) if capture appears imminent.

Private Behn Yahzee (Adam Beach) is taking a bath in a stream; as he tries to put on his clothing, Chick (Noah Emmerick) steps on his clothes and refuses to allow him to get his gear. Chick asks, "You know the difference between you and a Jap, Yahzee? That uniform—that's it. See, I know you people. I know what kind of slanty-eyed savage you are, boy." He cautions Ben about being alone in the woods by himself citing "I might just take you for a Jap." Ben inquires, "Are you going to let me get dressed, Chick, or keep demonstrating what an ignorant fool you are?" Chick kicks Ben and the two begin to fight. When the other troops step in to stop the fight and support Ben, Chick defends himself by saying "I thought he was a Jap who killed a Marine for that uniform. Damn injun looks just like a Jap don't he?" Ben speaks up, "I'm no damn Injun. I'm Navajo, of the Bitter Water People, born for the Towering House Clan." Sergeant Joe Enders (Nicolas Cage) argues, "But you do look like a nip. Next time you decide to take a bath, you let me know or I'll kick your ass." The scene ends when one of the soldiers calls Chick a "fucking shitbird" and walks away.

Elapsed time: This scene begins at 01:02:30 and ends at 01:05:57 (DVD Scene 17)
Rating: R for pervasive graphic war violence, and for language
Citation: *Windtalkers* (MGM Studios, 2003) written by John Rice & Joe Batteer, directed by JohnWoo

With Honors   CLASSISM/DISCRIMINATION

Harvard public-policy major Monty Kessler (Brendan Fraser) finds himself in a pinch when his thesis ends up in the hands of Simon Wilder (Joe Pesci), a resourceful vagabond living in the university library's basement. Sensing a meal ticket, Simon offers to trade pages of the essay for food and lodging. An unlikely bond forms between the pair, and Simon teaches the self-absorbed, overachieving Monty that there's more to life than book learning.

Arrested on a vagrancy charge, homeless man, Simon Wilder (Joe Pesci), has been bailed out of jail by Monty Kessler (Brendan Fraser), a senior at Harvard University. Wilder has managed to get his hands on the only copy of Monty's senior thesis and will not return it to him. Simon begs a young coed for a quarter to buy a newspaper; he takes the entire stack and tries to sell them to others. Simon asks the young lady, "Do you know what the greatest nation in the world is, don't you?" She answers "I hope it's the USA" but he responds, "Donation," with a chuckle. Monty follows, saying, "Mr. Wilder, I bailed you out, I think that entitles me to a conversation." Acting like a corner news barker, Simon yells, "Extra, extra, read all about it. Harvard student dies in freak accident—crushed by giant ego." Monty offers Simon five dollars for the remainder of the newspapers, which angers Simon who questions, "What do you see when you look at me?" Monty says, "A man." Simon argues, "No, you see a piece of shit, Harvard!" Monty responds, "I see a man who needs a home," to which Simon relates "I had a home. I had a warm place to sleep. 17 bathrooms and eight miles of books [he had been living in the basement of the Harvard library when Monty found him and reported him to the police]. I had a goddamned palace. You know why I need a home? Because of you. Because you looked at me and didn't see a man." The scene ends when Simon storms away.

Elapsed time: This scene begins at 00:16:39 and ends at 00:18:11 (DVD Scene 7)
Rating: PG-13 for language and brief sensuality
Citation: *With Honors* (Warner Brothers, 1994), written by William Mastrosimone, directed by Alek Keshishian

Without a Paddle   **HOMOPHOBIA**
Three friends leave their home in Philadelphia for a camping trip after their friend Billy's death. Their destination has special meaning, as Billy was fixated on going there to search for a lost treasure. Hoping to find some of the $194,200 of famed airline hijacker D.B. Cooper's money – rumored to be located somewhere in the wilderness – the men embark on the adventure of their lives.

Dan, Tom, and Jerry are on the run from two drug-dealing mountain men. They are half naked from an earlier altercation; each of them is in his underwear. Dan (Seth Green) is tired and begins to shout, "I'm out! I have spent the last, like, two hours within sniffing distance of a sweaty ball sack and a sweaty ball sack, and I'm out! I'm out!" Jerry asks, "What does that mean?" Tom answers, "I think it means he's out. Like, coming out. Like he's finally admitted, he's gay." The trio continue to argue about various things, including whether Dan has asthma or not. Dan argues that things could not get any worse than their present condition when a cloudburst begins. Dan and Jerry shiver underneath a rocky overhang, suggesting to Tom that he should join them so as not to die from hypothermia. Dan suggests that their "only chance is to huddle together. We gotta huddle our bodies together for warmth." Jerry states, "I, for one, choose death." Tom adds, "Interesting. One minute you mock my sweaty ball sack, and now you want to cuddle with it. You know, the whole huddle up thing is the oldest trick in the book; I've used it. It's just for getting a girl naked." [During a pause, the soundtrack plays "My mind's telling me no, but my body is telling me yes." R. Kelly's hit "Nothing Wrong with a Little Bump and Grind"]. The three begin to cuddle together and lay down on the ground. The three "spoon" each other and Tom states, "This never leaves the cave."

All is going well until Jerry and Dan begin discussing the sexiness of two women they came into contact with in a previous scene. Dan apparently begins to get an erection which causes Tom to freak out, screaming "Oh my God, Dano, how could you?" Jerry begins apologetically crying, "I'm so sorry. What happens in the cave, stays in the cave." Jerry complains that he is cold and tells the boys to come back to the huddle, but Tom lashes out, "not until he puts Jabba back in the hut." The scene ends when an unnamed mountain man (played by Burt Reynolds) pulls a rifle and yells "Freeze perverts" and marches them up the mountain with threats of shooting off their testicles.

Elapsed time: This scene begins at 01:04:00 and ends at 01:09:00 (DVD Scene 9)
Rating: PG-13 for drug content, sexual material, language, crude humor and some violence
Citation: *Without a Paddle* (Paramount Pictures, 2004) written by Fred Wolf and Harris Goldberg, directed by Steven Brill

X-Men   **OPPRESSION/DISCRIMINATION**
They are genetically gifted mutants – the world's newest, most persecuted minority group. Amidst increasing fear and bigotry, Professor Charles Xavier (Patrick Stewart) provides a safe haven for powerful outcasts like Wolverine (Hugh Jackman), Rogue (Anna Paquin) and Storm (Halle Berry). But can the X-Men triumph over Magneto (Ian McKellen) and his band of evil mutants?

Jean Grey (Famke Janssen) is testifying before a senate hearing regarding the subject of mutants living in the United States. The senate is preparing to vote on the subject of requiring mutants to be registered with the government. Grey begins by discussing when the mutant gene is first exhibited during puberty. She is interrupted by Senator Kelly (Bruce Davison) who questions, "Are mutants dangerous?" Grey suggest the question is unfair given the fact that anyone behind the wheel of a car can be considered dangerous. She continues, "Senator, it is a fact that mutants who have come forward and revealed themselves publicly have been met with fear, hostility, even violence. It is because of that ever present hostility that I am urging the senate to vote against mutant registration. To force mutants to expose themselves will only further…" The senator interrupts, "Expose themselves? What is it the mutant community has to hide I wonder that makes them so afraid to identify themselves?" He continues by describing different mutant powers including a young girl with the ability to walk through walls. "Now what's to stop her from walking into a bank vault, or into the White House, or into their houses [the audience in the gallery]? There are even rumors, Miss Grey, of mutants so powerful that they can enter our minds and control our thoughts, taking away our God-given free will. I think the American people deserve the right to decide whether they want their children to be in school with mutants, to be taught by mutants. Ladies and gentlemen, the truth is that mutants are very real, and they are among us. We must know who they are, and above all, we must know what they can do." The gallery erupts with applause to end the scene.

Elapsed time: This scene begins at 00:05:54 and ends at 00:08:00 (DVD Scene 4)
Rating: PG-13 for sci-fi action violence
Citation: *X-Men* (20th Century Fox, 2000), written by Tom DeSanto & Bryan Singer, directed by Bryan Singer

X-Men   **OPPRESSION**
They are genetically gifted mutants – the world's newest, most persecuted minority group. Amidst increasing fear and bigotry, Professor Charles Xavier (Patrick Stewart) provides a safe haven for powerful outcasts like Wolverine (Hugh Jackman), Rogue (Anna Paquin) and Storm (Halle Berry). But can the X-Men triumph over Magneto (Ian McKellen) and his band of evil mutants?

Senator Kelly (Bruce Davison) is boarding a helicopter amidst the cheers of hundreds of supporters who wish to rid the country of mutants. Once aboard, he is having a phone conversation with another senator: "Senator, listen, you favor gun registration, yes? Well, some of these so-called children possess more than ten times the destructive force of any handgun. No I don't see a difference; all I see are weapons in our schools." Once the call ends, his assistant questions the success of their plan by looking to the United Nations World Summit. The senator responds, "We're Americans, Henry. Let the rest of the damn world deal with mutants in their own way. You know this situation? These mutants? If it were up to me, I'd lock them all away. It's a war. It's the reason people like me exist.

Elapsed time: This scene begins at 00:29:53 and ends at 00:31:12 (DVD Scene 9)
Rating: PG-13 for sci-fi action violence
Citation: *X-Men* (20th Century Fox, 2000), written by Tom DeSanto & Bryan Singer, directed by Bryan Singer

You Don't Mess with the Zohan   **GENDER/STEREOTYPE**
Zohan (Adam Sandler), an Israeli counterterrorism soldier with a secretly fabulous ambition to become a Manhattan hairstylist, fakes his own death and going head to head with an Arab cab driver (Rob Schneider) – to make his dreams come true.

Zohan (Sandler) is having dinner with his parents when he mentions that he is not interested in continuing his counter-terrorism activities to "start a new life." He mentions "There's other things I can do besides war." His desire is to do "something more creative." Zohan's father argues that capturing terrorists is an "art;" he calls Zohan "a Rembrandt with a grenade." Zohan reluctantly tells his parents that he is interested in moving to America to become a hair stylist; his parents chuckle, and his father scoffs, "You? You *fagala*?" Turning to his wife, Mr. Zohan adds, "He's *fag—Faga*" and begins to make effeminate postures. Zohan declares, "I like hair. It's pleasant. It's peaceful. No one gets hurt." His father retorts, "Well, you're only digging that *fagala* hole deeper and deeper." Peering downward, he continues, "Hello down there. Hello in the *fagala* hole." He continues to make fun of him as the scene ends.

Elapsed time: This scene begins at 00:07:49 and ends at 00:10:29 (DVD Scene 3)
Rating: PG-13 for crude and sexual content throughout, language and nudity
Citation: *You Don't Mess with the Zohan* (Columbia Pictures, 2008), written by Adam Sandler, Robert Smigel, and Judd Apatow; directed by Dennis Dugan

REFERENCES

Bee, F. (1998). *Facilitation skills*. London: CIPD Publishing.

Cross, T., Bazron, B., Dennis, K., & Isaacs, M. (1989). *Towards a culturally competent system of care: A monograph on effective services for minority children who are severely emotionally disturbed.* Washington, DC: Georgetown University.

Day-Vines, N. L. (2000). Ethics, power, and privilege: Salient issues in the development of multicultural competencies for teachers serving African American children with disabilities. *Teacher Education and Special Education, 23*(1), 3–18.

Goldberg, B. (1997). Tailoring to fit. Altering our approach to multicultural populations. *ASHA, 39*(2), 22–28.

Goldberg, D. T. (2009). *Multiculturalism: A Critical Reader*. Los Angeles: Wiley-Blackwell.

Heron, J. (1996). *Co-operative Inquiry: Research into the Human Condition*. Sage.

Hyman, R. (1980). *Improving Discussion Leadership*. New York: Teachers College Press.

Isaacs, M. R., & Benjamin, M. P. (1991). *Towards a culturally competent system of care. Volume II: Programs which utilize culturally competent principles.* Monograph on effective services for minority children who are severely emotionally disturbed. Washington, DC: Georgetown University.

Jacobs, W. (2005). *Speaking the lower frequencies: Students and media literacy*. New York: SUNY Press.

Johnson, B. C., & Blanchard, S. C. (2008). *Reel diversity: A teacher's sourcebook*. New York: Peter Lang.

Lee, E. (1998). *Beyond heroes and holidays: A practical guide to K-12 anti racist, multicultural education and staff development.* Washington, DC: Teaching for Change.

Longerbeam, S., & Sedlacek, W. (2006). Attitudes toward diversity and living learning outcomes among first and second year college students. *NASPA Journal, 43*(1), 40–55.

May, S. (Ed.). (1999). *Critical multiculturalism: Rethinking multicultural and antiracist education.* Philadelphia: Falmer Press.

Merchant, D. (2008). *Lord save us from your followers: Why is the gospel of love dividing America?* Dallas, TX: Thomas Nelson.

Pope, R., Reynolds, A., Mueller, J., & Cheatham, H. (2004). *Multicultural competence in student affairs.* Los Angeles: Jossey-Bass.

Rotheram-Borus, M. (1993). Multicultural issues in the delivery of group interventions. *Special services in the schools, 8*(1), 179–188.

Sparks, D., & Singleton, G. (2002). Conversations about race need to be fearless. *Journal of Staff Development.* Retrieved from http://www.wmep.k12.mn.us/Posting/JSDSingletonSparks.pdf on 06/16/2009

Steinberg, S. (Ed.). (2009). *Diversity and multiculturalism: A reader*. New York: Peter Lang.

Sue, D. W. (2003). *Overcoming our racism: The Journey to Liberation*. Los Angeles: Jossey-Bass.

Torres, V., Howard-Hamilton, M., & Cooper, D. (2003). *Identity development of diverse populations: Implications for teaching and administration in higher education: ASHE-ERIC higher education report.* Los Angeles: Jossey-Bass.

INDEX

A

Anti-semitism
  Borat, 38–39
  The Chosen, 42–43
  School Ties, 92

C

Classism
  Beverly Hills Chihuahua, 34–35
  Dirty Dancing, 49–50
  Madagascar: Escape 2 Africa, 76
  With Honors, 104–105
Compulsory heterosexuality
  The Birdcage, 36
  GI Jane, 56
  The Hot Chick, 65–66
  In and Out, 67–68
  Little Miss Sunshine, 74
  The Next Best Thing, 81–82
  Saving Silverman, 91
  Swing Vote, 96–97
Co-optation
  Alvin and the Chipmunks, 27–28
  The Condemned, 44–45
  Dumb & Dumber, 50–51
  Finding Forrester, 53
  Freedom Writers, 55–56
  Head of State, 62–63
  Jawbreaker, 70
  Lakeview Terrace, 72–73
  Newsies, 80–81
  Pocahontas, 86–87
  September Dawn, 93–94
  Swing Vote, 96–97

D

Difference
  Coneheads, 45
  Daddy Day Camp, 47
  The Family Stone, 52
  For Richer or Poorer, 55
  Happy Feet, 61–62
  I am Sam, 67
  Lakeview Terrace, 72–73
  Lost in Translation, 74
  Racing Stripes, 88
  SLC Punk, 89–90
  School Ties, 92–93
  September Dawn, 93
Discrimination
  26, 300
  Benchwarmers, 34
  Beverly Hills Chihuahua, 34–35

Blazing Saddles, 37–38
Forrest Gump, 54
Gangs of New York, 56–57
Harold & Kumar: Escape from Guantanamo
    Bay, 62
Higher Learning, 65
The Jerk, 71–72
Jungle Fever, 72
Legally Blonde, 73–74
Philadelphia, 86
Pocahontas, 86–87
Racing Stripes, 88
A Raisin in the Sun, 88–89
Rush Hour 3, 89
South Park: Bigger, Longer, & Uncut,
    94–95
Sweeney Todd: Demon Barber of Fleet
    Street, 96
Underworld, 100
Who's Your Caddy?, 103
With Honors, 104–105
X-Men, 106–107
Dominance
  Blazing Saddles, 37
  Dangerous Minds, 47–48
  Dazed and Confused, 48–49
  Dr. Seuss' Horton Hears a Who, 50
  Finding Forrester, 52–53
  Mona Lisa Smile, 78–79
  Pocahontas, 86–87
  Saved!, 90–91
  Swing Vote, 97–98
  Walk the Line, 101

E

Ethnocentrism
  300, 25–26
  American History X, 28–29
  Coneheads, 45
  Fools Rush In, 53–54
  For Richer or Poorer, 55
  Gangs of New York, 56–57
  A Good Woman, 57–58
  Hotel Rwanda, 66
  It's a Mad, Mad, Mad, Mad World, 69–70
  Rush Hour, 3, 89
  Underworld, 100

G

Gender
  Beauty Shop, 31–32
  Billy Elliot, 35–36
  In and Out, 68–69

It's a Mad, Mad, Mad, Mad World, 69–70
Made of Honor, 76–77
Mona Lisa Smile, 79
An Officer and a Gentleman, 84–85
Parenthood, 84
Philadelphia, 85–86
The Stepford Wives, 95–96
You Don't Mess with the Zohan, 107–108

H
Heterosexism
   The Birdcage, 36
   The Next Best Thing, 81
Homophobia
   Ace Ventura, Pet Detective, 26–27
   American Beauty, 28
   As Good as it gets, 30–31
   Be Kind Rewind, 33–34
   Cursed, 46–47
   In and Out, 67–68
   Philadelphia, 85–86, 105
   Without a Paddle, 105–106

I
In-Group
   The Ant Bully, 30
   The Bee Movie, 33
   Bringing Down the House, 40
   A Bug's Life, 41–42
   Cursed, 46–47
   The Family Stone, 52
   Jawbreaker, 70–71
   Lords of Discipline, 75–76
   Saved!, 90–91
   Tyler Perry's Madea's Family Reunion,
      77–78
Invisibility
   Dr. Seuss' Horton Hears a Who, 50
   Maid in Manhattan, 78
   Not Another Teen Movie, 84
   Sweeney Todd: Demon Barber of Fleet
      Street, 96

O
Oppression
   The Bee Movie, 32
   Boyz n the Hood, 39–40
   A Bug's Life, 41
   Cursed, 46–47
   Equilibrium, 51–52
   Mr. Woodcock, 79–80
   Welcome to the Dollhouse, 101–102
   X-Men, 106–107

Out-Group
   25, 300
   The Bee Movie, 33
   Benchwarmers, 34
   The Birdcage, 363
   Boyz n the Hood, 39–40
   Coach Carter, 43–44
   The Color Purple, 44
   Dirty Dancing, 49–50
   The Family Stone, 52
   Heavyweights, 63–64
   Higher Learning, 64–65
   Maid in Manhattan, 78
   The Next Best Thing, 80
   Tyler Perry's Madea's Family Reunion,
      77–78
   Varsity Blues, 100–101

P
Power
   Braveheart, 40
   Dirty Dancing, 49–50
   Equilibrium, 51–52
   Glory, 57
   Guess Who's Coming to Dinner, 59
   Hairspray, 60
   Mr. Woodcock, 79–80
   Newsies, 80–81
   Varsity Blues, 100–101
Prejudice
   Blazing Saddles, 37–38
   Hamlet, 2, 60–61
   Higher Learning, 64–65
   Swing Vote, 97–98
   To Kill a Mockingbird, 98–99
   Twelve Angry Men, 99
   Windtalkers, 104
Privilege
   21, 25
   Braveheart, 40
   I am Legend, 66–67
   We Were Soldiers, 102

R
Racism
   American History, X, 28–29
   Blazing Saddles, 37
   Glory, 57
   Harold & Kumar: Escape from Guantanamo
      Bay, 62
   Hotel Rwanda, 66
   The Jerk, 71–72
   Lords of Discipline, 75

A Raisin in the Sun, 88–89
South Park: Bigger, Longer, Uncut, 94–95
To Kill a Mockingbird, 98–99
Who's Your Caddy?, 103–104

S
Sexism
Anchorman: the Legend of Ron Burgundy,
   29–30
Black Knight, 36–37
The Color Purple, 44
GI Jane, 56
Higher Learning, 65
North Country, 82–83
An Officer & a Gentleman, 84–85
She's the Man, 94
The Stepford Wives

Social justice
The Contender, 46
The Great Debaters, 58–59
North Country, 82–83
Tears of the Sun, 98
We were Soldiers, 102–103
Stereotype
Beauty Shop, 31–32
Freedom Writers, 55–56
The Next Best Thing, 81–82
The Producers, 87–88
Twelve Angry men, 99
You Don't Mess with the Zohan, 107–108

Printed in the United States
By Bookmasters